CAREERS FOR YOU

Careers for You

Erma Paul Ferrari

ILLUSTRATED BY CLIFFORD JOHNSTON

Abingdon Press
New York • *Nashville*

CAREERS FOR YOU

Copyright MCMLIII by Pierce & Washabaugh

Library of Congress Catalog Card Number: 53-10007

F

SET UP, PRINTED, AND BOUND BY THE
PARTHENON PRESS, AT NASHVILLE,
TENNESSEE, UNITED STATES OF AMERICA

Contents

CHAPTER ONE

It's Your Career

THERE is something in the very word "career" which makes you think at once of major league material. The "career man" or the "career woman" must do spectacular things, like building bridges or digging up lost civilizations or serving in Congress, we are likely to think. And so they do.

But a career is also a *job*, or a series of jobs, which may or may not be spectacular. The cleverest scientist will tell you that his career consists largely of performing one job after another, the jobs being in his case long and sometimes unsuccessful experiments. The anthropologist who travels to far places also has many very routine jobs to perform as he searches for evidence of life in ancient times. He hires labor, keeps records, and arranges for transportation.

In short, the outstanding worker in any vocational area is called upon to do a lot of everyday chores which, though they may be dull in themselves, are very necessary to his career.

On the other hand, what we usually refer to as a "job" may be in its own right a very satisfying and important ca-

7

reer. I know of a carpenter in a community who is one of that town's most valuable citizens, because he works so skillfully with his hands and tools to meet a need in the community. In the space of a half-hour he can give a set of sagging steps a new look. With a little more time he can "dress up" a room with a built-in china closet or picture window. He could build a house with his hands and his tools, but most of his adult life has been spent just fixing things. A neighbor once remarked that this skillfull man had kept their town from falling apart, literally.

That carpenter is a career man. He brings high skill to the performance of his job, and he knows that he is making a contribution to the community. If a job meets those requirements, it is a career—whether the worker builds bridges or bakes cakes, and both accomplishments are important.

To know that it is possible not only to hold down a job and earn a living, but also to carve a career out of that job, gives this business of career selection a more interesting perspective. Almost anyone can get a job, some kind of job, and earn a living. But there is a very significant difference between holding down a job and building a career. And that difference does not have too much to do with the nature of the work done, but with the way the worker regards his work and the interest and skill with which he tackles it. One may reach for the stars from many different levels.

So your lifework may or may not call for great learning; it may or may not take you to far places; it may or may not get your name in the papers or lead to an appearance on television. But the job of your choice, well done, will be your career, if that's the way you feel about it. And that is why it is so very important that you find the right job for you.

This matter of the choice of a vocation is one of the three most important decisions that you will ever be called upon to make. Between now and, let us say, your twenty-fifth birthday, you will in all probability make those three decisions; and they will chart the course of your life. Incidentally, they must be your own decisions, made under the guidance, perhaps, but never the dictation of someone else. At these three important points there must be no backseat drivers. These choices are strictly your own business.

Perhaps you have already made the first and most vital of all decisions—that which will determine your relation to God. For an alert, straight-thinking young man or woman this must not be a sentimental decision only. It must be made in an awareness—borne out of your training, personal experience, and observation—that a life without God is aimless, puzzling, and incomplete. This decision will not be definitive in the sense that it will be inflexible and unchanging. On the contrary, a true religious faith helps us to walk forward, growing mentally and spiritually as we meet each new experience in fellowship with God. Our religious faith gives us a place on which to stand; a frame of reference, the scientist would say. Whatever form your vocation may take, it will be unsuccessful in any real sense, and unsatisfying, unless you are aware that your career belongs first to God, from whom all skill and knowledge come.

The second decision will center around your choice of the person whom you will marry. That the "one and only" may be just around the corner is an intriguing idea, for marriage, homemaking, and family-building are great stuff. For that very reason they involve not only deep love, but wisdom and intelligence of a high order.

It may surprise you to learn that there may be a direct

relation between your date life and the third basic decision you will make, the decision in which we are at the moment directly interested, namely, your choice of a lifework.

We shall consider in this book some of the questions which face us as soon as we begin to think seriously about our lifework: What do I want to be? Where can I get information about careers? How can I make a success of my career? Will my personality fit my job?

These and other questions are answered in the light of the help which we get from our Christian faith. And that is very important. For the young man or woman who prepares to enter the world of work with what is sometimes called the "Christian philosophy of vocation" is headed for true success in life's great adventure.

The term, "Christian philosophy of vocation," means simply that to God, and therefore to the Christian, all honest, useful work is sacred. It means that the mechanic, the man or woman in business, the secretary, the teacher, the artist, the engineer, and all Christian workers who dedicate their careers to God, use that career not only to make a living but to help build a Christian world.

This philosophy means, too, that the Christian worker tackles his job, whatever it may be, with an interest and an enthusiasm which the young man or woman who looks forward only to a pay check and the next day off cannot share.

The Christian, you see, is building a life as well as a career. And he lives his faith as forcefully at his day's work as he does at public worship. That is not always easy, as we shall see later, but the effort to make one's job a Christian medium gives zest to life and brings immeasurable personal satisfaction.

These three—a religious faith, a happy marriage, and a

satisfying vocation—are, with good health, life's best gifts. And the encouraging truth is that they are largely at our command. To be sure, they are not the gifts of Santa Claus. Life is not a pushover. There would be little to challenge us if it were. And your vocational life is no exception.

But in these days of preparation for their lifework, the Christian young man or woman living in America holds the ball. Our country is the greatest in the world in opportunity for self-development. American students have the best educational facilities available to them, many without cost. And there lies ahead of them a vast world of interesting and profitable vocations.

Twenty-four thousand jobs, all different from one an-

other, are a lot of jobs, and that is the number from which
young America may select a lifework. The very fact that
American life is economically so complex creates a problem
in selection. On the other hand, such a wide choice practically guarantees that you can find the job that will be just
the right spot for you.

The expression "square pegs in round holes" is a cliché.
But there are still far too many square pegs "sweating it out"
in round holes. Sometimes "sweating it out" is a noble attitude. What can't be cured must be endured, our grand-
parents used to say. This may be good Spartan philosophy
but not much fun. The fact of the matter is that most vocational misfits can be cured, or, better still, they can be
avoided in the first place. Young people sometimes find it
necessary to do some job experimenting, but the more time
and effort they expend on searching and preparing for the
right job, the less wasteful job-flitting they will have to do
later on.

Square pegs get jammed into round holes for many reasons
—through ignorance of the multitude of vocational possibilities available for every talent; through lack of guidance;
sometimes because young people are in a hurry to get to
work, and so float into the first job that comes along; and
sometimes because they harbor the false notion that a vocation for which they have obvious talent or aptitude lacks
the prestige of some other type of work for which they may
not be fitted at all. Whatever the causes, misfits are unhappy, sometimes tragic figures in their miscast roles.

Now getting the right job is important for more reasons
than may occur to us when we first begin to search for our
place. It is unfortunate enough to have to spend our precious
working hours at something we thoroughly dislike, but there

is a lot more to a job than the actual work we do. Our life-work influences greatly, and sometimes determines, where we live, our standard of living, our circle of friends, our marriage, our home life, and, most important of all, our personal growth. There are some jobs, for example, that demand residence in a particular section of the country, or in a foreign country. There are jobs that make it impossible to establish a permanent home and form lasting friendships in the home community. There are jobs which pay so poorly that workers cannot maintain the proper standard of living. There are jobs which pay well but are hazardous to health or personal safety. There are jobs which contribute to the mental and spiritual growth of the worker, and there are others which do not. It is the by-products of a job that are often just as important, or more so, than how we put in our time on that job.

Right here seems to be an appropriate place to flash a red light before that girl who regards a job as only a stopgap to marriage and therefore not worth being choosy about. Her desire to meet and marry a man worthy of her love and to establish with him the home of her dreams is commendable. But the notion that because she hopes and expects to marry, she might as well take any job that comes along and never mind any serious preparation, is dangerous. In the first place, marriage is not always forthcoming. There are far too many girls in business and industry today who, pending marriage, stepped into a job which had little appeal, only to find themselves, in a few years, sentenced to it for life. And year by year they are growing duller and thereby less attractive. An interesting and interested personality gives any girl, or boy, for that matter, a head start on the road to romance; and just the right job is a big help in personality building. It's not too difficult to fall in love with a happy, enthusiastic girl who is doing what she really likes to do in the way of a job and getting a thrill out of it. Such a girl is almost sure to have both intelligence and charm. Furthermore, the job you really can get excited about has romantic possibilities in itself. There are qualities of mind, similar tastes, and kindred talents and skills which arouse mutual attraction when boy meets girl in a vocation that both have entered because that is where their interests lie.

So even though you have no ambitions to be a career girl, even though your goal is a home of your own with a fine husband and children, plan your future around a vocation that suits you and for which you are suited. If you do not marry, you will have a career that will bring great satisfactions and many joys. If you do marry, you will be a better wife and mother for having cultivated your own talents and skills; and you will have added security in the event of a family emergency which makes employment desirable or necessary for you. Furthermore, the time will come when your children will have grown up and left the home. Then a vocational interest keeps life interesting and rewarding.

There are many avenues open to young men and women today for finding their places in this stimulating modern world. And in finding a lifework that will be worth what you have to bring to it, you will find yourself; and all those by-products which are so fascinating in prospect will be yours—vocational advancement, an income of your own, good friends, far horizons perhaps, worth-while service to society, and the thrill of pursuing life's great adventure— your career.

You are, you hope, headed for "Operation Success." But remember, as you strive, that it is far more important to *be* a success than to *gain* success, and there is a vast difference between the two. It is not difficult, in this favored land of ours, to make money, to become a public figure, to go far in business and the professions, and otherwise to gain what is commonly called success, if one is willing to concentrate on those goals to the exclusion of many other activities. Nor is gaining success necessarily to be condemned. But to *be* a success involves far more, as many a disillusioned millionaire has testified. True success is the total of many qualities. Talent and ability to be sure, but added to those are courage, love, sympathy, broad interests, good cheer, and strength of character.

Joyce Kilmer stated that abiding truth in a beautiful eulogy which he wrote for a gallant friend.

> Because it was old Martin's lot
>   To *be*, not *make*, a decoration,
> Shall we then scorn him, having not
>   His genius of appreciation?
> Rich joy and love he got and gave,
>   His heart was merry as his dress;
> Pile laurel wreaths upon his grave
>   Who did not *gain*, but *was* success.[1]

---

[1] From *Trees and Other Poems* by Joyce Kilmer. Quoted by permission of the publisher, Doubleday and Company, Inc.

CHAPTER TWO

Is It Worth Your Life?

AFTER one of his incomparable recitals Fritz Kreisler was approached by an effusive young woman who exclaimed to him, "Oh, Mr. Kreisler, I would give my life if I could play like that!" She was momentarily silenced when the great musician replied quietly, "My dear young lady, that is just what I gave."

Your career, whether it is chosen with intelligence and purposefully followed, or entered upon haphazardly, the "easiest way," will demand your life—just that. Actually, of course, no one will step up to you with such a proposition when you are offered a job; but when you make your vocational choice you are saying to yourself, if you are a young man, and often, too, if you are a young woman, "I am willing to give the next forty or more years of my life in return for certain things that I expect to get from this vocation, or this job, or series of jobs."

The minimum number of working hours required of you will be determined by the nature of the job; the maximum number may know no limit. Few people gain professional or vocational prominence who limit their working day to seven or eight hours, five days a week, and you may well find yourself working or studying at your job far beyond a forty-eight hour week. So in actual time consumed, your career will demand most of your life. It will demand also your physical energy, your mental powers, your talents, skills, and abilities. That is a sobering thought.

What do you want from life? Another way of asking the same question is, for what would you be willing to trade your life, or the next forty years of it? Your choice of a career should be influenced very definitely by your answer to that question, for one career will guarantee one set of returns, and another career another set.

For what have men and women in your own time and throughout history mortgaged their lives? You can run through the list very quickly: money, power, fame, prestige, self-expression, "easy street," permanent satisfactions, service to mankind. You can suggest other objectives as you look about you and as you recall man's progress through the ages. Some of these goals are commendable and some are not. Some pay in full for "value received." Others do not. Some are worth the precious lives put into them. Others turn out to be poor investments. Men and women have too often worked and sacrificed and bargained to gain an objective, only to discover at the end of their career that it wasn't worth what they paid for it. Others, and history is the brighter for their contribution to life, may not have made the grade in material gains, but they found at the age of retirement that they had been giving their lives for something precious all the while—something that could not be evaluated in terms of those things which are commonly considered the criteria for judging success.

You have a right to expect from your occupational career the highest rewards, if you are prepared to bring to it all your capacities for success. What are those rewards? If the career is worth your life, it will compensate you in several areas.

First, in *adequate financial returns*. Money is not the most important reward of a career, but it is important. At this stage of your preparation you may be straining at the leash to get to work for that coveted pay check, and that is understandable. And it cannot be too large, you are thinking. That, too, is understandable. But you will be very wise to keep the financial aspect of your career in its proper place. Money should be the last consideration in your career-building program, and not the first, for it can be pretty shoddy stuff. This bit of advice is not as unpalatable as it may sound to you on the first reading, once you think it through. You are intelligent enough to know that no bank account is worth broken health, days and months and years of boredom on the job, loss of self-respect, the necessity for pushing other people around, a frustrated personality, or a weakened character. So you see, the phrase, "Money isn't everything," is more than a timeworn bromide. It is packed with truth. That young man or woman who has an eye out for the main chance, whose working philosophy is, "The world is my oyster," or who is looking for the easy "buck" and the "fast" dollar, is headed for dismal, self-destructive failure. The records of thousands of people who have built their careers along such a pattern are there for all to see.

It is not too difficult to get to the top in American life. But to the top of what, and how? You can reach the top of an honorable vocation by study, intelligent planning, and work. And at the end of such a career you will look down, clear-eyed, over the long trail up and review with satisfaction the fun, the challenges, the barriers, the achievements, the setbacks, and the helping hand you gave to other climbers. Or you can sometimes get to the top through intrigue, compromise, or by pushing others ruthlessly aside. From the top of such a heap the view is not pleasant, as many bitter men and women have admitted, to themselves if not publicly.

You are looking forward to receiving adequate financial returns from your lifework, and you will receive them if you prepare yourself to fill a need in the community. And money will assume its proper place in your life if you train yourself to think always in terms of people rather than things.

A second reward of a thoroughly worth-while career should

be the *opportunity to express yourself*. Now that does not mean that you are going to write the "Great American Novel," though perhaps you will, or produce a masterpiece on canvas, though you may do that too. It does mean that your career will give you an opportunity to do something that you can do well, from which you can obtain personal satisfaction, and in which you may take merited pride. Your job may call for artistic talent, mechanical ability, effective salesmanship, an orderly mind, nimble fingers, fluency of speech, or other qualities. It will give you the opportunity for expressing yourself if it is suited to you, and if you have prepared yourself to fill it satisfactorily, for then you can bring your best to it.

Closely related to self-expression is *personal growth*. Sometimes this is a matter of learning more and more about a job; sometimes it calls for developing by-products of a job. The physician or the nurse, for example, has no problem in finding opportunities for learning more and more about their professions, for there is always more and more to learn. The industrial worker whose job is confined to performing the same mechanical operation hour after hour and day after day may find it necessary to cultivate his mind and spirit off the job. A group of students working with Students-in-Industry reported that the most common complaint of the young people beside whom they worked one summer in a large manufacturing plant was not poor wages or long hours or bad working conditions, but the stifling monotony of their days. Our industrial system demands that many, many thousands of people be employed at work which dulls the imagination and deadens the spirit with changeless routine. Such terms as "self-expression" and "personal growth" are just about meaningless on such a job. For these workers it is doubly important that leisure time be employed to the best possible advantage, that they may cultivate other interests. We shall have more to say about this difficult labor problem, for many young men and women must face it.

Finally, and above all things, the career which is worth your life must *make some contribution* to the world in which you live. Christian young people, headed for the world of business, industry, and the professions, must face frankly and without naïveté the fact that there are careers, often highly profitable careers, which contribute to the ill-being, even to the degeneration, of society. The liquor industry, unwholesome forms of entertainment, the production and distribution of second-rate materials—all these and other enterprises of the same type are bidding for youthful talent, and most of them pay well. A placement bureau, a vocational counselor, a casual friend, well-meaning perhaps but without the Christian yardstick, may at one time or another point out the financial attractions of a career which would ask you to lower your banners. At that point some rather serious thinking and a long look ahead and backward are in order. What does this business, this job, contribute to my fellows? What has been its history over the years? What will it do to my own character as I give myself to it? Despite the fact that it may not violate the laws on the statute books, is it highly ethical? Does it make life more beautiful, easier, more interesting and worth while for the people it seeks to attract? In short, is it worth my life?

Christian faith compels us, and it is likewise a high privilege, to make vocational choices on the basis of service to the world—to dedicate, if you like, talents, skills, and aptitudes to God. Not "What has life got to give me?" but

"What have I got to give life?" is the Christian's query as he considers what his lifework is to be.

Young people have many different areas of choice, within the church organization and outside in the secular world, to which they may be divinely called. There are world frontiers waiting for the touch of God's hand through the talent, the courage, and the intelligence of youth. To be sure, the frontiers of today differ in nature from those which challenged explorers of continents or builders of empires. But frontiers are still with us, and they are more important than discovery, exploration, and empire-building, for they are the frontiers of human life—of the body, mind, and spirit of men and women and boys and girls. Your generation has before it only a partially explored route to world peace, a route fraught with hazards and barriers more formidable than any which faced Balboa. If Christians cannot blaze that trail, you may be sure that non-Christians will never do so. The frontier of scientific research and achievement, directed to the welfare of the world, calls for the keen intellect of consecrated young men and women. There must be some members of your generation who, either as private citizens or as political officeholders, will dare to tackle corruption in government, on local and national levels. There must be those who will provide Christian management in industry, and others who will chart the course of labor. The frontiers of social and economic needs beckon to American youth as they set out upon their lifework. Housing, recreation, educational standards, medical care—these terms have become platitudes in the political lingo of our day, but they represent the tragic needs of millions of Americans. And Christian youth, working in every area of our country, must do something about them. It is for your generation to determine whether the divorce rate will continue to climb, or whether American homes shall be happy, comely, stable, and Christian. From your generation must come the professional leaders of the church, that it may be an increasingly effective instrument for helping men and women and boys and girls to live the abundant life.

It is not necessary to travel afar to discover world frontiers today. They are borne in upon us, to be attacked on the home front with intelligence, courage, and high devotion. So it is that you may be called of God to serve at the desk, the counter, the wheel, the workbench, or behind the plow —at home or in the market places of the world. To such a career you may unhesitatingly give your life; and you will find it again in permanent satisfaction, inner contentment, the thrill of striving, sometimes with success and sometimes without, and the blessing of God.

CHAPTER THREE

Will You Suit the Job?

WE DO NOT reach a decision regarding our lifework by sitting down with the *Dictionary of Occupational Titles* and pondering over all 24,000 jobs listed therein! In fact we do not start with the job at all; we start with that fascinating person, ourself.

The traditional question asked by the vocational counselor is, "What do you like to do?" Likes and dislikes enter into the choices we make, to be sure; but perhaps you are not aware of liking to do any one thing more than another, or your preferences in the way of hobbies and leisure-time activities may run to several interests. Furthermore, there are almost invariably several different job areas for which you may be fitted by natural endowments, whether you realize it or not. Self-analysis must go deeper than likes and dislikes for it is qualities of mind, body, temperament, and character that point the first arrows to satisfactory careers. Nature gave you these fundamental qualities to start with, to be developed to your advantage.

So your first question in the process of discovering yourself might be this: What kind of person am I *mentally?* Most adolescents pass through a stage of indifference, if not downright laziness, when it comes to work, but you have presumably outgrown that period, so your high school or college grades should be a fairly accurate gauge of your attitude toward study and learning. If your grades are satisfactory, or above average, the chances are that you can make good in any vocation that interests you, although the intellectual demands of even the learned professions vary somewhat. If your grades are not high for no more serious reasons than that you have been coasting along, content with just getting by, now is the time to do a quick-change act and tackle those textbooks with an eye to the future, when your school record will really count. And that record, by the way, *will* make a difference, in two very important ways. In the first place, until you have acquired some job experience, your teachers and school advisers are the only ones who can tell a prospective employer whether or not you are intellectually industrious and can buckle down to a job calling for some brain power.

In the second place, unless you have acquired habits of study in school, you will find the traveling very rough in a job that calls for concentration and intellectual application. It's smart to acquire those habits during school days.

If, despite reasonable effort, you find your studies very difficult, or if school is pretty much of a struggle and you long to be at something which you can tackle with enthusiasm, you need not feel that all the good jobs are automatically closed to you. But face frankly the fact that careers which call for college and graduate work, and usually serious study on the job as well, are not your cup of tea. There are other careers in which you can make your mark. However, all young people, en route to a lifetime vocation, should study the mental demands of occupational fields with their own capacities in mind.

The mental demands of an occupation are determined in several ways. No one of the following tests is definitive. There are exceptions to all of them. But in general you can be assured that an occupation calls for a mind which can apply itself readily to serious study if:

1. The salary paid in the occupation is high.
2. The occupation has high standing in society.
3. The period necessary to prepare for it is long and includes advanced education.
4. The occupation involves a variety of duties.
5. The work involved calls for decision and judgment in its performance.

This means that even though you may be clever and gifted along some lines, unless you are prepared to dig into those books for the long pull, you will have to discard any thought of a career in most of the professions, science, business administration, engineering, teaching beyond a certain level, and a job in any large executive capacity, to mention a few.

But without even one degree after your name, you may

be a highly successful salesperson; you may have just the touch needed to work successfully with people in any one of several different occupations; you may enter the important and growing field of food preparation and distribution; you may establish and run your own business; you can earn your living, and a good one, with some creative or manual skill; and so on. The more education the better, but a high degree of learning is not the deciding factor in many worthwhile vocations. All vocations, however, require *intelligence*.

Now what do we mean by intelligence? Psychologists agree that it is not a single quality of mind, but is made up of several factors and abilities, as you have already discovered if you ever took an intelligence test to determine your I. Q. The most important of these mental abilities have been grouped into five general classifications. Glance through the list below and you will quickly see that they have a bearing upon one's choice of a vocation.

Where do you fit in these categories of mental abilities?

Verbal meaning—the ability to understand ideas expressed in words

Space—the ability to think about objects in two or three dimensions

Reasoning—the ability to solve logical problems

Number facility—the ability to work with figures

Word fluency—the ability to write or talk easily, or both

We are not ready to scan definite areas of work here, but it may interest you to match some occupations with which you are familiar and some of the mental abilities in this list. One very successful worker may have one ability and be almost completely lacking in another. But everyone, to be successful in a vocation that is worth while, must possess at least some of these mental abilities.

There is another aspect of your mental capacities to be ıonsidered as you evaluate yourself, and that is your mental health. In the light of reports of widespread mental breakdowns among young people, and the far too common reliance upon liquor, narcotics, and other "props," our mental health deserves serious attention as we prepare for the rigorous world of work ahead. The more challenging a career is, the more responsibilities it entails; and all types of work are occasional sources of worry and failures. If you have had the usual experiences of normal young people, you have probably had your quota of emotional upsets. How you were able to handle yourself in such circumstances gives a clue as to how you will react to larger responsibilities and problems in an adult world. So let's take a look at our behavior pattern. Of course Robinson Crusoe had no behavior problems, for his social contacts were limited. But as soon as we move into a world of parents, neighbors, teachers, pals, and casual acquaintances—even strangers with whom we come into contact fleetingly—our behavior pattern, that is, how we react to our environment, comes into existence. That means it starts developing almost the moment we are born.

Granted that all normal people are at times plagued with fears, ignoble impulses, and emotions difficult to manage, the person of healthy mind is ordinarily cheerful, self-possessed, and interested in life about him. He finds pleasure in the many small things which in the aggregate comprise the lives of most of us. He seeks "escapes" from the injustices of life by bettering those conditions as he finds them in his own spheres of activity, be it home, school, work, or social life. His "props" are work, play, service, and, if he is a Christian, prayer.

Much of the unhappiness and unrest which sensitive young people experience arises from the many questions which life presents that seem to them unanswerable. There are sorrows, failures, injustices that cannot be explained; but you will be wise if you do not try to fit all the pieces of life's puzzle together at any particular period. It takes a long time, and sometimes a lifetime, for many of these questions to be answered. Young people can develop mental and emotional stability which will see them through if they will prepare themselves as best they can for the years ahead by cultivating their Christian faith through worthy companions, church activities, and private devotions. And by letting life as they live it, with courage and zest from day to day and from year to year, provide some of the answers to problems that baffle them.

Your own emotional problems may arise from some serious catastrophe in your home or family, or they may spring from what you believe is some inadequacy on your part—failure in school, lack of popularity and social success, some physical handicap or ill-health. If you become too anxious about your troubles, you will be tempted to take refuge in one of two very common attitudes. The psychiatrists call them the "fight" and the "flight" attitudes. The "fight" attitude is kid stuff. The small boy down the street rebels against discipline and either puts up a howl or punches a playmate. But grown-ups can be pretty childish, too, so they also become belligerent and "won't play." Did you ever see a high-schooler deliberately try to break up a class session or disrupt a club because he or she was disgruntled about something? Another favorite "fight" reaction is to be sullen and stubborn. Of course these attitudes deceive no one; and, more serious, they are encouraging a behavior pattern that, unchecked, means failure in any occupation that calls for self-control; and most of them call for a lot of it.

The "flight" attitude is even more serious. The tabloids and too much modern literature are full of stories of people who are trying to run away from themselves or their environment through the media of liquor, narcotics, and a frenzied search for a good time—all symptoms of their "flight" attitude toward life. Less serious "flights" are those into daydreaming or a withdrawal from people and activity. When these habits become so excessive that they result in "queer" personalities, they reflect a serious mental illness.

Young people who have chronic fears, anxieties, and inner tensions should, first of all, see to it that they avoid excesses of any kind in their attempt to smother their worries. Such excesses do not solve any problems; they only create more problems. And there is always help to be had. Sometimes we can help ourselves. Dr. William Menninger, one of the most prominent and successful modern psychiatrists, tells us that "there is convincing proof that if we really gave it a chance, love could be the cure for all evil, for hate is the main cause of evil. It is *the* emotion that gets human beings into almost all their difficulties." That statement is a powerful plug for the Christian belief that perfect love casts out fear, and without fear the mind is healthy. "Be of good cheer, I have overcome the world," Jesus told his worried, harrassed disciples; and he *had* overcome the world, with love and service. His followers are still overcoming fear, hate, selfishness, greed, loneliness, and failure by loving and serving others, as they tackle life's problems with intelligence and vigor.

So much, in capsule form, for your mental capacities. Equally serious must be your attention to your *physical* state. So the next question is: What kind of person am I physically? If you have normal health, you enjoy the energy of youth; but even physical characteristics differ from one young person to another, and jobs likewise differ greatly in their demands upon one's physical resources. Some call for muscular strength, some for unusual powers of endurance; others necessitate irregular hours, travel, night work, indoor or outdoor living. Some jobs, and they are frequently good jobs, involve close association with noise, dirt, dust, grease, and oil—to which even healthy people may be allergic.

Once again you can run through the occupations with which you are familiar and note those in which the worker's physical reactions matter a great deal, not only when he is a young worker, but also when he gets into the "older worker" category.

It is being neither weak nor a "sissy" to admit that you cannot hit on all eight cylinders without nine hours of sleep every night, or that the doctor discovered a heart murmur when he examined you in the gym last fall. Facing the situation frankly is sensible and may guarantee you a rugged life for the next half century, even though the hundred-yard dash or a strenuous tennis match is out for the present. It pays to look yourself over physically before you prepare for a career that will make unusual physical demands upon you. Nor do any of you huskies who are in perfect condition want to burn out an efficient new engine with lack of care.

These first two areas of self-analysis, mind and body, have

an enormous amount of influence upon your answer to the third query: What kind of person am I *socially?* Now, you are doubtless thinking, we are getting somewhere! Personality! That's what we all need to make the grade! What is personality, and can we do anything about the one we inherited?

Personality is your complete person—your speech, your dress, your appearance, your disposition, temperament, and character. It is, furthermore, what everybody notices about you first—a sort of advance representative—and it is also what you put to work for yourself first. Two young persons, equipped equally well in training and skills, apply for the same job. The employer can make his selection on only one basis, and the top personality wins out.

Not long ago a study was made of seventy-six large corporations in our country to find out the reasons for job failures. The survey came up with the astonishing fact that only 10 per cent of the young workers who were fired lost their jobs because they were lacking in skills and ability. The remaining 90 per cent lost their jobs because of some personality defect. Personality, obviously, has priority rating.

Lest some of us entertain the notion that only the "life of the party" has personality, it may be well to check off some of the things which personality is *not.*

Personality is not *noisy.* It isn't the amount of chatter we can produce, or the depth of our lung power that counts in a personality contest.

Personality is not all *glamour,* or *oomph.* It goes much deeper than that; otherwise, what passes as personality on short acquaintance wears pretty shabby with the passing of time.

Personality is not *imitation*. Granted that all of us could do with a little improvement, and that we can change our appearance and our habits, fundamental patterns cannot be changed successfully. Changing your hair-do and tackling that poor posture is all to the good and may affect your personality, but it will not affect the real you very much. And if nature did not cut you out for the chatterbox type of girl or the strong, silent type of fellow, do not try to make yourself over along a pattern that just will not fit. You will only succeed in being a phoney and in detracting from your own personal attractions, of which, you may be sure, you have your quota.

The obvious starting point in evaluating a personality is with what the people whom we meet notice first; namely, our appearance. As Woodrow Wilson said in describing what he thought was his homely face, "My face, I don't mind it, for I am behind it; it's the folks out in front that I jar!"

So here you come, marching up bravely, more or less, to the desk of the personnel manager in search of a job. What does the fellow "out in front" see?

It would almost seem unnecessary to ask modern young people to check through such a list as the following. But a girl entered my office not long ago in search of a job, dressed in rumpled skirt and loafers which had long since seen their best days.

Grade yourself honestly on the following points:

Is my posture erect?
Is my hair-do or my haircut neat and becoming?
Are my teeth in good condition?

Are my nails scrupulously clean?
Are my clothes neat?
Is my make-up appropriate?

To be erect, neat, and dressed attractively and appropriately does not cost much in dollars and cents, but it pays large dividends in poise, self-confidence, and social and vocational success.

Next comes the question, What does the fellow out in front *hear?* One of the faults commonly found with young people on the job is that they cannot use English correctly or without undue reliance on slang. If you lived in a country where the so-called common people learned a dialect at home rather than the classical form of their language, you would, like the students in those countries, be very proud when you had mastered your native tongue. These students have reason to be proud, for education is hard to come by in most of the countries of the world. Not so in America, where a free educational system has made us indifferent to its priceless opportunities. Our high-school graduates, and often our college graduates, cannot, so say the employers, construct a grammatically correct letter, or carry on a conversation with anything like an adequate vocabulary.

It may be a new idea to you that an early point of attack in personality improvement should be your vocabulary, but it is a good idea. It is not necessary to strive for eloquence; but that girl to whom everything, conversationally at least, is "awful" or "nice" or "keen" is likely to be a very dull person, and all the make-up in the world will not hide such a personality deficiency. And that fellow whose stock reply to any statement is, "You can say that again!" or "You're not kiddin'," is not going to get very far in a career. An employer of my acquaintance who hires young people by the score remarked that he could always identify the students of foreign birth who came to him for vocational counseling, because they spoke such perfect English!

Increasing one's vocabulary is really fun, as attested to by the popularity of the vocabulary tests in some widely read periodicals. It might be revelatory for you to try one someday. Be proud of the English of Shakespeare and Milton and the King James Version of the Bible, and prouder still of the fact that you share the language of such greatness. Learn to use this most potent ally to vocational success. It will interest you to know that a cross-country survey of recent graduates of high school, made in an effort to determine wherein these young workers felt that their school courses had failed them, or wherein they themselves had failed to make the most of what was offered them, turned up some significant reports. One was that 33 per cent of the young people polled said that they wished very much that they could speak better! So, as one young man wrote on his paper, "Get hep to your English!"

We have made a good start, but there is far more to personality than appearance and sound effects. Underneath the smooth paint job there must be an engine that performs efficiently, in fair and foul weather, on good and bad roads. In other words, What sort of person am I socially and emotionally?

It is possible to lump all the elements of emotional stability and social success into one consideration: *How do I get along with others and with myself?*

At the risk of overdoing the self-test idea, we submit another easy one that will help you locate or identify personality problems, if any. Stand off and look at yourself without rationalization or excuse. How many of the following questions can you answer in the affirmative?

Do I like people, on the whole?
Can I get along well with my friends and family without quarrels?
Do I enjoy the company of both boys and girls?
Do I usually have a friendly attitude toward the world?
Do I avoid trying to excuse my failures or blaming them on someone else?
Am I enthusiastic?
Am I courteous and well-poised?
Am I always willing to do my share?
Am I taking my place in church activities?
Am I relatively free from worry and inner tensions?
Am I free from suspicion and jealousy?
Can I profit from my mistakes?
Can I overlook or laugh off unkind rebuffs and snubs?
Am I cultivating daily devotions?

The more "Yes" answers you have, the higher your score. The "No" answers reveal those areas in which some remedial work is required. Whatever the nature of your emotional difficulty, there is intelligent help available to you. Some of the most eminent doctors, psychiatrists, pastors, teachers, and clergymen have published sound professional advice. You will find the titles of inexpensive pamphlets listed in the bibliography at the end of this book. The most successful people in the world have taken advantage of such professional help with their personality problems, so do not be ashamed to face yours intelligently.

While you are aware of certain personal flaws and try to do something about them, do not make the mistake of worrying too much over them. That way lies more trouble. It is easy to become both self-conscious and self-centered if we concentrate too much on ourselves. You can determine to attack those weaknesses every time they crop up, with the punch of an all-American tackle. But between times, do not dwell on them. Give your good points their share of attention too.

On the positive side you doubtless have personality traits that suggest aptitudes for certain vocational fields. Those we have already considered are "musts" for almost all successful workers. But the type of personality you have, or your temperament, often determines the general nature of the work for which you are best fitted. For example, that young man or woman who works better and more contentedly alone than with others is probably more interested in working with ideas than with people. Their bent is toward the creative or artistic—science, agriculture, craftsmanship, literature, research. (Even in these fields, however, most workers must be able to "sell" their services or their wares.) On the other hand, the extrovert is the successful sales person, social service worker, teacher, athletic director, young people's worker, pastor, lawyer, politician, or public relations man. The outgoing personality fits well in occupations that call, first of all, for direct contact with people.

There are other personalities which cannot do their best work under close supervision, or under outside pressure. This is not necessarily a weakness, but simply a matter of natural temperament. Such people would obviously not be happy or efficient trying to meet the deadlines in a newspaper office, in many advertising agencies, in some merchandising areas, or in the average business office. They are more successful when they can set their own pace.

All these and other phases of personality have some bearing on the type of work to which you should direct your attention in these days of preparation. And it is encouraging to remember that there are worth-while vocations today for all normal personalities.

Personality at its finest is evidence of character. It identifies you as the real thing, a thoroughbred, or as just a veneer of the genuine article. A personality, no matter how attractive on short acquaintance, which is not sustained by honesty, loyalty, kindness, and courage, soon disappoints.

A questionnaire sent out not long ago to several thousand employers throughout the United States asked, "What are the most essential qualities you seek in your employees, listed in the order of their importance to your business?" The employers who received that questionnaire were practical, realistic businessmen. Their standard of success was the success of their business, nothing else. They selected and promoted young men and women on the basis of the contribution those young people could make to the business. That being the case, they might, it is reasonable to suppose, have listed such things as efficiency, skill, personality, and technical knowledge. But those employers knew the score. The questionnaire said "most essential," and so by far the greater number of them voted for honesty, loyalty, and dependability, in that order. They well knew that if their employees possessed strong character, they would almost without exception possess, or be able to acquire, all the by-products of character that add up to occupational success.

CHAPTER FOUR

Will the Job Suit You?

I HAVE had many young people say to me when discussing their vocational future, "But I don't know what I want to be." And they were frequently a bit puzzled or disturbed about what seemed to them to be their lack of any conspicuous talent which would direct them straight toward their one and only vocational spot. Perhaps a budding young genius in the neighborhood was already well on the way to a career in science, or the girl next door was a "born" musician. There are such people of course; although the "born" musician was probably likewise "born" to other vocations as well, for nobody is "cut out" to be a teacher, a doctor, a decorator, or even a great musician, to the exclusion of every other occupation. The normal person does possess talents and abilities that equip him for certain types of work. That is why the painter is often an equally talented sculptor, and frequently a musician in the bargain; and a clever mechanic is "handy" also with plumbing, electrical apparatus, carpentry, and other manual skills. One reason for this occupational flexibility is that there are what the experts call "job families," which resemble one another in skills and abilities required for their performance and in physical conditions of work.

No young person with whom I have ever talked failed to drop a clue, in response to a few questions, as to their possible place in a job family. I recall the son of a not very successful farmer who, at eighteen, could see nothing ahead of him except grinding work from five o'clock in the morning until after dark at night on a farm that was ill-equipped and mortgage-ridden, largely because of poor management. It was a grim outlook; but this young man, eager as he was to get away from the farm, made it clear as we talked that he felt a kinship to the soil. A trip to town was a welcome diversion, but he was always glad to get back to broad acres, poor as they were.

We considered his problem for some time. Finally the way was opened for him to spend one year at the state agricultural college, and today he operates a highly successful greenhouse on a few acres of the once large farm that had been such a burden. This was one of several occupations for which his background, experience, and interests had equipped him. If his aptitudes had included a bent toward the mechanical, if he had enjoyed repairing and tinkering about the farm machinery, or if his major interest had been in the farm livestock, more than actually working on the land, another job family would have been in order.

Similarly, that girl who has a flair for clothes, who knows when they look well, and why, has a fairly large job family from which she may make an occupational choice: designing, dressmaking, costuming, decorating, buying, or some other phase of merchandising in the clothing field.

It is encouraging to know, too, that young people of ability and intelligence are usually, within reasonable limitations, versatile. They can step successfully from one job family to another. They can learn to do a variety of things and bring the needed skill to their performance.

So having determined what type of person you are mentally, physically, and socially, you may next throw the spotlight outward and sweep it across the vast vocational world to discover what skills and abilities you may add to your natural equipment to secure a job in a field which interests you.

Since this idea of job families is basic, it will be helpful to scan them more closely, with your own occupational future in mind. Does any one of the following ring a bell?

Artistic	Public Service	Recording
Musical	Technical	General Clerical
Literary	Personal Service	Public Contact
Farming	Managerial	Cooking
Entertainment	Computing	Child Care

These are the family groupings found in the *Dictionary of Occupational Titles* issued by the U. S. Employment Service.

This classification, you will note, is concerned with the skills, talents, and interests of an individual, and not with a definite job or a business or profession within which that skill and talent may be used. You will think at once of several occupations that fit into these job families. Here are a few examples:

MANAGERIAL JOB FAMILY

Office Manager
Plant Superintendent
Department Store Head

Personnel Manager
Building Superintendent
Shop Foreman
City or Town Department Head

´Likewise, some of the jobs listed in this Managerial family
are to be found in other job families. Many of them are
found in the Public Contact family, the Technical family,
the Public Service family. All this duplication and over-
lapping demonstrates how wide the range of appropriate
job choices is.

We shall consider definite jobs within these job families
in Chapter 8. Meantime, the first step in finding out what
you should be studying and planning for in preparation
for your lifework is to decide, tentatively, in what job
families you feel at home. That involves discovering your
interest pattern and building on it.

In your own group of friends you can doubtless spot
several different areas of interest. There are those whose
methodical minds get a good deal of satisfaction from
the commerce courses in school—bookkeeping, stenography, filing, computation. Their interests and aptitudes
point rather definitely to clerical work. It is important for
such students to remember, however, that there is often
a wide and interesting choice in the type of office requiring
such work. There are many types of records, and some are
concerned with far more interesting subjects and details
than others.

In any group there are always a few who obtain their
greatest pleasure in working with and for people. Here are
the future ministers, nurses, social service workers, therapists, teachers, athletic directors, public relations men, and
so on.

You may find patterns that point to literary, artistic, or musical interests; others that give promise of successful careers in the scientific and mechanical fields; others in working with plants, animals, or minerals.

Phil's favorite study in high school was mechanical drawing. He had an orderly mind, neat habits, an eye for balance and good design, and agility with a pencil. The job family to which Phil belonged seemed to be Technical, and there the choice of careers was a large one—architecture, drafting, printing, layout, automotive design, and many other technical fields in various industries and professions such as publishing, aviation, and engineering.

Very likely Phil could also fit into the Artistic family in some capacity. His concern at the moment was how he could develop his aptitudes and skills to best vocational advantage. He had to decide where he belonged within the job family and how to prepare for that general job area. Architecture was his final choice. An interview with his school counselor raised the first hurdle. His school grades over the three years of high school indicated that he would have to plug harder at his mathematics and that he would have to take the advanced mathematics course offered in high school if he really meant business about becoming an architect. College, too, was practically a "must."

During the early years of his preparation, Phil discussed his ambition with an architect of his acquaintance and visited the workrooms of his friend's firm, where he saw draftsmen on the job, some of them doubtless headed for the top. His interest in his projected career grew with each visit.

Phil had been as definite about his vocational future as it is usually possible to be in prep school. He had decided to what job family his personal preferences, his grades in school, and his native skills and aptitudes pointed. He then had made a rather definite choice from among the occupational possibilities within that family. Then he had determined what the career of his choice demanded in the way of education, training, special knowledge, abilities, and other requisites; for his choice must be influenced not alone by personal taste but also by a consideration of the practical opportunities available to him for preparation. That was not the end, by any means. Phil discovered that he must add much more to his equipment—he must learn to draw from memory, to develop his imagination with ideas for building and designing, and it would be to his advantage to read and study the best professional literature in his chosen field. Since his choice of architectural fields was home design, he familiarized himself with building materials and how to put them together. He delved into the mysteries of plumbing, lighting, and masonry, even before he was actually required to do so in the course of his formal architectural training. There is a lot more to a house, Phil discovered, than a smooth-looking design.

Here was Phil's formula for discovering whether a job would suit his aptitudes and skills:

interests + talent and ability = job family
opportunity + personal choice = occupation within job family

A definite choice of jobs is not necessary during school or college days, but it is highly desirable to think about likes and dislikes, the activities one enjoys, hobbies, favorite school subjects, and so forth. These interests are not fixed, of course. They may change completely or develop from some general area to something more specific. But thinking about them now will start you off well, if not on the definite path toward your life career, at least in the right direction.

Just for fun, take pencil and paper and jot down those things you have done which you have really enjoyed doing. Include every activity that interested you and gave you pleasure. One girl's list included camping, singing, and working on the school paper. A college freshman's list read: riding and taking care of horses, counseling at a boys' camp, and chemistry.

Be sure that the basis of your selection is *personal interest* and not just something that was easy. It might have been both, of course, but once in a while something is interesting that comes hard! Based on personal interests, to what job families do you seem to belong?

In your study of your interests, skills, and abilities, the following pointers will be of help to you.

1. *Do not belittle what comes easy,* if it really interests you and you are good at it. If you are a "whiz" at camping and so at home with the out-of-doors that you are prepared to meet practically any emergency, don't say, "Oh, anybody can do that!" Indeed they cannot, but you can, and that's the important thing. That aptitude may steer you to the forestry service, an interesting job in horticulture, the lumber industry, topographical surveying, the sporting camp business, to mention a few of the possibilities.

A sixteen-year-old girl whom I knew was a genius with children. She could keep any number of them busy, disciplined, and happy with apparently no effort. When I told her one day that she was already headed for a satisfying and profitable career in one of several areas, she was surprised to the point of disbelief. That was too easy! "There's nothing

to handling a bunch of kids," said she. I pointed out that perhaps there was nothing to it for her, but that I could mention several people who were both helpless and hapless with such a bunch. That talented girl had been thinking about her lifework in terms of something strange and difficult. That a career was practically in sight because she "had a way" with children was a new idea.

There are promising fields of work today for practically all talents. So if your favorite diversion is cooking, writing, debating, tinkering with machines, working in the laboratory, and even baby-sitting, don't depreciate your skill; dignify it, for it may spell your destiny.

2. *Take advantage of part-time jobs to help you discover vocational interests and aptitudes.* The girl who has a yen for the nursing profession, for example, may have her somewhat

vague interest in that vocation firmly fixed in her future plans by becoming a nurse's aid in the local hospital, or she may have it dispelled in a hurry. Now is the time to find out. A Sunday-school class is a fine place for actual teaching experience, even though the conditions of work are different, and frequently more difficult, than those in the secular classroom. Saturday work in a store may bring to light an aptitude for some phase of merchandising. Even a soda jerker discovers that he or she likes to serve the public or that he does not, and the baby sitter that she has the needed patience and ingenuity for handling children or that she has not. The fellow who sells a phenomenal number of tickets to some school event could probably sell with equal success to consumers in the business world.

Study your failures on the part-time job and determine their cause. Were they due to immaturity, lack of experience, or basic ineptitude? If the first, your failure was part of the growing-up process and should be regarded as a lesson learned the hardest but often the most enduring way— by experience. If a conscientious try was made without marked success, the chances are that area of work is not for you, except as it serves as a profitable interlude between school and your final job. Your judgment of any job, however, should be based on the work as a whole and not on some unpleasant episodes or a few dull duties. The most glamorous position in any occupational field turns up some difficult, unpleasant, and dull chores. It's the over-all picture that counts.

3. *Make your own choice intelligently.* You may be well advised by parents, teachers, counselors, and other adult friends, but the final choice of a life career must be your own; for it's your life. Sir Walter Scott was forced by his

unimaginative lawyer-father to study for the bar. Fortunately for the world, however, Scott, while drudging away at a vocation in which he had no interest, cultivated an avocation which had always fascinated him, namely, a study of the romance of Scottish history. Scott is not remembered as a legal advocate, but as the greatest writer of historical novels that the world has yet produced.

Now it may well be that you would make as successful a teacher as Aunt Cora, who attended the state teachers college in your area and entered upon a career which was obviously the right one for her. Furthermore, as may be pointed out to you, "The girls in our family run to teachers." But you may be the first girl in your family who runs in quite another direction. At any rate, find out for yourself. Even though you might make out fairly well as a teacher, you want to do more than "make out." You want your choice to be your dream job, and it will be if you spend some time and effort on its selection.

4. *Choose your school courses with your occupational future in mind*, insofar as that is possible. Occupational misfits usually start on their tortuous life journey fairly early, frequently when they are first confronted with the necessity for making choices of studies from the school curriculum. At this point it is probably too early for a student to say definitely, "I want to be a nurse, a doctor, a secretary, or a businessman." So if you are not sure of your vocational choice, keep your high-school course as general as possible. Do not limit yourself to business subjects, for example, just because a pal signed up for the commerce course, or because that seems to be the shortest route between you and a job. Do not narrow your high-school preparation to the point where you will be completely ill-equipped if you should find,

in your senior year, for example, that the vocation which interests you calls for some mathematics, or science, or a language which you have not had. Your school counselor or principal can direct you in keeping your choice of studies as generally comprehensive as possible.

5. *Don't be a job snob.* Perhaps the widespread educational opportunities in America have given rise to the notion that everybody who "is anybody" must go to college, or have a white-collar job. Sometimes college is not possible, and sometimes it is not desirable, if a student is not college material. And a white-collar job is often not nearly so satisfying as a blue-jeans job. When a young man with a pair of clever hands, who might have been a top-notch artisan, finds himself stifled in a very dull office because he had the erroneous idea that an office "position" held prestige and a skilled worker's job did not—a promising life is ruined. And when a young woman who has the knack for styling hair and working with people becomes a stenographer, because her family regards the stenographer's job "refined" and that of the beauty operator not quite worthy of their daughter, another tragedy is in the making.

This mistaken notion about the relative dignity and importance of one set of jobs over another accounts for more occupational misfits and maladjustments than any other factor.

A young woman and her brother built up one of the most successful boat-building businesses on the Atlantic seaboard because the boy "stuck to his last." He turned down a proffered job in a local bank, and stayed in his father's shop building dories for local fisherman. He worked in overalls; his hands became calloused; but he was creating something that he knew how to create, and he enjoyed every minute of his working hours. Today he continues to build dories, but his large boatyard turns out handsome yachts as well, and his business-minded sister manages the office.

You can reach the top in any trade; and a skillful machinist doing well what he enjoys doing is a happier, healthier, and more highly respected member of the community than a frustrated stockbroker who is a misfit in his work, college graduate and white-collar worker though he may be. And the machinist is likely to enjoy larger financial returns as well. There is dignity in any job for which one has prepared and in which the worker is happy.

The Welsh carpenter who had learned some lessons more important than grammar had this to say about his work:

> I don't know right where as His shed may ha' stood,
>   But often as I've been a planing wood
> I've took off my hat just when thinking of He
>   At the same work as me.
>
> . . . .
>
> And I'll warrant He felt a bit proud like I've done
>   At a good job begun.
>
> . . . .
>
> So I comes right away by myself with the Book,
>   And I turns the old pages and has a good look
> At the text as I've found, as tells me as He
>   Were the same trade as me.[1]

---

[1] "Jesus, the Carpenter" by Catherine Liddell.

CHAPTER FIVE

How Much Education?

YOU MAY very well know some high-placed executive in your community who rose from office boy to president or general manager of a large company as the result of hard and intelligent work. But this type of American "success story" is becoming rarer and will probably disappear altogether with the present generation of older executives. Today the top positions are filled by young men and women who equipped themselves with the necessary education or training before they entered the company. They were never office boys or messenger girls. When workers without education or training are promoted, it is usually to clerical jobs consistent with their educational background. They rarely advance very far, and they are sometimes bitter when the company overlooks them entirely and brings in young people from the outside to fill the best jobs.

You probably do not need to be told why your grandfather, perhaps, got a job at sixteen and was his own boss or head of his small company at thirty. In the first place, the world of business was very different in grandfather's day from our complex economic system. The grocery, hardware,

drygoods, and drug store were small and owned by one
person or possibly a firm of two persons. Even the factories
and mills were comparatively small. It was common practice
and not difficult for a man of ability to establish his own
business. And so every town and city in America had its
quota of successful merchants and industrialists, who very
frequently had little formal education. Likewise, the local
banker, perhaps a high-school graduate but sometimes not,
entered the bank as a clerk, became teller, then cashier, and
finally president or treasurer. The only competition was
within the bank itself, and ability, not education, was the
requirement.

Similarly, most of the mills and factories were local industries, founded and carried on by men of the community
who promoted boys and girls from within the ranks of the
workers.

Today, if your community is typical, many of the grocery
stores are branches of large chains of stores, most of them
country-wide enterprises. If you live in an industrial area
this also may be true of some of the drug, hardware, and
clothing stores; it is almost certainly true of the movie
theaters and one or two hotels, and possibly of the banks
and many of the manufacturing companies. Under such
conditions, not only are the opportunities few for a person
to establish his own business, but to be promoted by ab-
sentee ownership to a position near the top, without advantage of education or special training, is practically impossible. The "big jobs" go to the college graduates who
come directly into the head office of the company, not to
local boys and girls who man the small branches of the
industries or stores.

In the second place, the competition for the good jobs is keen because there are far more people of education and training looking for them. Many more young people go to high school and college today than did thirty or forty years ago, and employers, who do not have to select from among those who dropped out of school early, are naturally looking for the best.

And finally, modern industrial and business techniques call for educational specilization. A young man or woman, bright and able though he or she may be, cannot fit into the average office or industry or store where the need is for stenographers, machine operators, trained salespersons, buyers, accountants, comptrollers, artists, laboratory technicians, public-relations men and women, workers in personnel, draftsmen, electricians, designers, traffic managers —to list only a few of the thousands of specialists in the labor market today.

That situation leaves the young person without education or training with a rather bleak employment outlook, unless he prefers to develop a skill such as those used in the building trades, in industry, and the transportation fields. In the larger cities, however, union demands must be considered. Even the skilled trades are not so easily entered as they once were. Apprentice training in industry is practically closed to young persons under eighteen, and high-school graduates are given a priority rating. In some of the largest cities a young man must have a member of his family engaged in a skilled trade or the union demands a long apprenticeship at half the union wages. Of course a college education, and usually graduate work leading to an advanced degree, is essential for most of the professions—for doctors, psychiatrists, scientists, teachers above the elementary school level, and the most accomplished lawyers and business administrators.

With that information in hand, the record of school dropouts will not surprise anybody. What happens to them? Assuming that they leave school because, for one reason or another, they want to get to work, do the jobs they get justify their decision?

Before getting into statistics, we might briefly review some of the grievances reported by the drop-outs themselves. Tom, at sixteen, had no trouble getting a job in a local establishment as stockboy. Twenty-five dollars a week looked like "big money" after a childhood of deprivations. For six months Tom was content. He was able to buy his clothes, pay board at home, and indulge in a luxury or two. But about the seventh month Tom began to get restless. He had no intention of remaining a stockboy all his life, so what was ahead in his company? Investigation and inquiry turned up the brutal answer, "Nothing!" Not one to give up easily, Tom pounded the pavements of his city during his noon hours, and questioned friends and acquaintances about possible employment. One prospect offered two dollars more a week than his present job paid, but no other inducement. Two years have passed, and Tom is now back at school; only this time it's night school and it comes harder.

Joan felt justified in quitting high school to take a job in a local factory, for financial aid was needed at home. Her educational ambitions were not encouraged by her parents, despite the fact that she was a good student and hoped some day to teach. Because she was alert, her piecework at a stitching machine paid fairly well. But a business slump hit the small textile plant, and Jean was the first to be let out, as the youngest and oldest usually are. Even in the best of times employment for teen-agers under eighteen is anything but steady. So Joan became an unhappy drifter, going from job to job. After a year she made a valiant effort and managed to get back to school, with a part-time job that helped out a little at home. In about three years' time Joan will be in a position to help substantially at home, and she will have a position that will not only pay a good salary but bring her personal satisfaction and social prestige.

Unfortunately the case histories of most school drop-outs do not reveal the happy endings of the stories of Tom and Joan. Most of them, for one reason or another, never go back, even though they regret their action. Most of them flit from job to job, looking for something with "a future" but never finding it. "I'm not old enough"; "I haven't a high-school diploma"; "They took somebody who graduated in my old class"; "The unions won't let me learn a trade," they report.

Although the reason for their predicament seems clear to them, strangely enough most of these young people never do anything about it. They have lost the habit for study and concentration; they just don't want to go back to school, hoping, like Micawber, that something will turn up. They get into a mental rut and give in to what seems inevitable. A survey made recently in an American city of average size revealed that of 524 boys and girls between the ages of fourteen and nineteen who had dropped out of school, one fifth of the nineteen-year-olds, one third of the sixteen-seventeen-year-olds, and one half of the fourteen-fifteen-year-olds had no jobs.

In many states it is against the law to employ young people under sixteen years of age for full-time work, and only

unscrupulous employers will do so. It is also against the law
to employ minors in hazardous occupations where they are
exposed to injury from machinery, lifting weights, and other
heavy labor. Obviously an employer trying to circumvent the
law in order to get cheap labor is not going to give any young
worker a square deal. On such a job the employment outlook becomes still more grim. And before you protest with
understandable self-confidence that "accidents wouldn't
happen to me!" you should be reminded that in three
heavily industrialized states of our country there were nearly
five thousand serious occupational accidents in one year to
workers under eighteen.

Yes, the fellow and girl who stay in school, at least
through the secondary school, get all the breaks—in job
opportunity, in the nature of the work they do, and in wages.
There are a few exceptions to the following statement, but
in the great majority of cases this is true: *The amount of
money one earns rises in direct proportion to the amount
of education one has.* So the college graduates with advanced degrees earn the highest salaries, followed by the
college graduates, the high-school graduates, and down to
the school drop-outs, who earn the least.

You will probably think at once of someone you know
whose career contradicts this rule. It is true that certain
highly skilled workmen (like diamond cutters) in an uncommon trade receive high wages. Workmen in hazardous
occupations like deep-sea divers and window-cleaners on
skyscrapers can command wages all out of proportion to
their educational background. Geniuses and highly gifted
people can also, and men and women in business can make
huge profits if they have very uncommon business ability
and offer a product or a service for which there is a heavy

demand. But despite these exceptions, it is still true that education "pays off" in the size of your salary check.

Granted that all these reasons for remaining in school are sound, you may still feel that your reasons for wanting to quit school are sounder. After all, advice is so easy to dish out to other people; but you have a problem, and quitting school is the only way to solve it. We don't know what your particular problem is, but may we have three guesses?

1. You want to get to work and earn some money.
2. You find school hard, or uninteresting, or both.
3. You have an emotional problem with teachers, students, or possibly at home.

Did we hit your case? If not directly, probably close to it, for interviews with thosuands of drop-outs bring out one of the above, or a closely related problem, that turned them against school.

If the trouble is money, a part-time job may be the answer, and also managing better with what you have. A young college friend of mine was having rough going financially trying to stretch a very small weekly allowance to cover necessary school supplies, tickets to college activities, frequent trips to the snack bar, movies, and the innumerable "extras" that can never be foreseen. Certainly school is not much fun if every small pleasure has to be passed up for lack of cash. Marie got so blue that she was seriously ready to "look for a job" at the end of her freshman year. But apparently she took time to think it over, for I recall the Saturday afternoon, in the college library, when she came up with a cash account based on a few weeks' expenditures as she recalled them.

That very week, for instance, her entire allowance had gone to the snack bar, and by Wednesday afternoon! Better management was part of the answer to Marie's problem; plus a baby-sitting job occasionally that gave her an opportunity to study, after Junior had gone to bed. And Marie's budget and complexion both improved with fewer snacks.

Often, as in Joan's case, there is a real financial need at home. If a girl or boy has a good mind and is intellectually ambitious, it may be desirable to go to work and attend school at night. This is hard work, for it means holding down two jobs and running the risk of getting discouraged under the extra load. Of course, such double duty makes unusual demands on health, too; but many young people are doing it, knowing that their goal is worth the effort.

Some communities or community organizations, like the Rotary and Kiwanis Clubs, have scholarships or other forms of financial aid for students who can profit from it.

By far the largest number of young people quit school at the legal age because they just "don't like school." It is, they say, hard, or dull. Is school really dull, or are you using that "flight" avenue again to escape a few solid sessions with books? Jim wasn't interested in French or history. In fact he was bored in most of his high-school classes, so he quit school and got a job as trucker's helper on a delivery van. After six months, Jim really knew something about boredom, changeless routine, long hours, exacting customers and employers, and no future!

Courses sometimes can be shifted, if you decide honestly that your vocational future can be built more solidly around one or two courses that do interest you. And you can manage to carry the less interesting required courses, if you make the sensible decision that it's the thing to do.

You may be convinced, for example, that English themes are not your dish and won't help you earn a dollar. But it just *could* be that you may some day have important letters to write, reports and estimates to prepare, a speech to make, or that you must understand the written words of somebody else. It's a pity to pass up the opportunity to learn how to handle your language effectively, and so handicap yourself for life.

Having turned over a new leaf, you may even have the pleasant experience of the girl who explained, still surprised at her discovery, "When I began to try to prattle French just for the fun, it *was* fun!" Keeping in mind that you will be earning your living for the next forty years or so, four years of high school is a very short period in which to prepare for it.

It isn't reasonable to expect that all studies will be equally interesting; but if schoolwork is difficult, here are some tips that have proved helpful to many students. After all, you expect to do your work, in whatever occupation you select, the most efficient way. School is your career at the moment, and these suggestions come from the efficiency experts. I will cite them briefly, to be adapted to your own situation. They will work, if you give them an honest trial.

1. Have a time and a place for study and stick to them. The time (now this is going to hurt a little!) should be before dates, dinner, and diverse duties—not after you have done everything else you think you have to do.

The place can be barn, library, or attic, so long as you can be alone and physically comfortable. Do not have radio, television, or a member of the family present, except maybe the dog, if he will keep quiet. And you are "out" to callers, in person or by telephone. Studying in the same place every day is a good way to acquire the "concentration habit."

2. Don't do all your studying at one sitting. An hour probably should be the maximum at a time. Budget your studying, however, so that every subject gets its share of attention. You will know which one needs the most.

3. Actually study when you study. Don't cheat by daydreaming, grumbling, munching crackers, doodling, or playing with Fido.

4. Aim to get your work done as quickly as you can without sacrificing efficiency.

5. Write down your assignments in class so you won't forget them and have to telephone to a pal—a forbidden interruption.

6. Use your textbook as a tool, and as efficiently as a carpenter uses his plane or a scientist his test tubes. Everything you need *is in that book*. Read it, and find out what is there. It may be math, science, history, or economics. Your textbook is your guide. Be sure that you make use of all its helps.

7. If your assignment is for reading, make an outline

of its major content and study your outline. Then, if the text has questions, give yourself a test with those questions.

If your assignment calls for memorization, then memorize, a bit at a time. Any fellow who can memorize football signals and any girl who can learn a complete initiation service for a club or a part in the drama society play, can learn the conjugations of a French or Latin verb—one tense at a time, of course.

If your assignment calls for problem-solving, then tackle each problem by these steps.

a) Write out facts given in the problem.

b) Make sure you know what is called for.

c) Review all processes and facts you have had previously.

Remember, if the problem is in the book, you have the facts with which to solve it. Somewhere in those printed pages you have your directions. Just now, the teacher is the boss and your job is that assignment. Don't let it lick you.

Try to account honestly for your failures, because the reasons for them are significant. Did you flunk a course because of a heavy date schedule, too much time on the athletic field, or too frequent sessions with television? Did lack of interest hold you back? The latter is by far the commonest reason for failure in school; not lack of mental capacity. Many a boy who flunks Latin can take an engine apart and put it together again, which the brilliant student of the classics might not be able to do. An engine interests some boys, while Latin interests others. Nevertheless, the fact must be faced that some subjects which may not be interesting to you now, are necessary or desirable in furthering your career. I remember Jane, who walked off with all the honors when it came to writing English themes but who was bored in her physics class, a study which she also found very difficult. But Jane stood by one year of physics because she made up her mind that a knowledge of some of the principles of that universally used science ought to be part of the equipment of any well-informed person. Today Jane is on the staff of a top-notch periodical; and when she is called upon to review or to rewrite an article on science, she does not have to spend hours "boning up" on it. She is not completely out of her element.

Any student headed for a career in a worth-while area of work knows very well that few vocations are built upon the foundation of "snap" courses in school. Difficult subjects are difficult because the careers they prepare for demand keen intellects and an understanding of difficult subject matter or of complex processes. For that very reason the courses themselves and the jobs they prepare for, directly or indirectly, are usually as interesting as they are difficult, once you put your shoulder to them.

But perhaps your reasons for wanting to drop out of school are personal. You aren't popular; you didn't make the basketball team; you changed to a new school and feel shy and strange; your teachers don't like you.

These are very real problems to many young people, and they are not to be laughed off. Let's think about them un-emotionally, as though someone else rather than you were involved.

First, although it may be distasteful to admit it until you have done some pretty serious thinking, the truth is that slamming the door on school will not seal your problems up in the schoolhouse. They will ooze through like genii and follow you wherever you go. Most employers are more exacting than your least sympathetic teacher, and if you are really unpopular at school, you are likely to be unpopular at work for the same reasons. If you suffer from shyness, you will find any place of employment much stranger than school, where at least you are accustomed to your environment and know your way about.

This leads to the second step in solving your problem the intelligent way. Start with yourself before you decide to run away from your surroundings.

We have already had something to say about social success. Quietly and patiently cultivate one or two friends and your circle will grow. Learn to do something really well, like playing tennis, strumming a banjo, or swimming, which will serve as a social asset. These are superficial attractions, to be sure, but they will give you poise and open the way for discovery by your associates of your real worth. And be sure you are trying to be popular with the right crowd which will be worth the effort. Some acquaintances are not.

Turn your attention to your studies, for the time being, rather than to yourself and your environment. It is quite true that some teachers are more sympathetic than others, but the teacher who does not recognize earnest effort and pupil co-operation is rare indeed.

If you have a school counselor, a teacher, pastor, or adult friend whose opinion you value, talk over your case with him. Tell him the whole story and do not try to cover up any of your worries. Just talking about them will help, and you will probably receive sound advice as well. If by chance your parents want you to leave school, or have no opinion one way or the other, have them talk to your counselor too. And you might profit from a rereading of Chapter 3. Above all, do not be in a hurry about achieving success, gaining popularity, or overcoming your handicaps. Achievement takes time in any area of life, and a well-earned diploma is much more important to you than a second-rate job.

There is evidence enough to convince the most prejudiced doubter that high school pays off in dollar wages. But it has values of far more importance than potential earnings.

With a good high-school record behind you, your range of occupational selection increases a hundred times. Each year the number of employers in every field who refuse to consider applicants without at least a high-school education increases.

Again, the more education you possess, the more job security you will have. The untrained and uneducated are the "last hired and first fired," because their services are almost always the least needed.

Your high-school experiences and training will give you poise and self-confidence, not only on your job but in the community as well. Education adds to the prestige with which you are regarded.

Finally, you will be a more valuable citizen and more capable of making a contribution to democracy, because your mind has been trained to think clearly and to tackle a variety of problems with intelligence. You will likewise be a more effective Christian. The ignorant person is not ordinarily an effectual witness for his Christian faith, even though he may be respected personally for his sincerity and admired for his character. But the Christian young man and woman of education are doubly well equipped to face the world of science, politics, and social problems with intelligence and balance, because they have studied the wisdom of the ages and have seen this wisdom used and enhanced, as Jesus used and enhanced it, to serve mankind.

Most of the arguments in favor of high school apply equally to a college education, and for many young people even more. We already know that for an increasing number of occupations college is either required or highly desirable. Nevertheless, there are many high-school graduates who can not, and many who should not, go on to college. Most institutions of higher learning screen their applicants so carefully and maintain such high entrance requirements that it is no simple matter to gain admission; and to make the grade a student must almost of necessity have been in the upper half of his high-school class, scholastically speaking. Colleges also take cognizance of a boy's or girl's spirit and purpose throughout prep-school days. College aptitude tests also enter into the competitive picture. Young people can no longer ordinarily select the college of their choice. The colleges do the selecting. So it is that nonstudents should not try to go on, and probably could not anyway.

There are also many young people of alert mind and high capabilities whose vocational aims would not be served by a college education. (Incidentally, it behooves a student to find out as early in his high-school career as possible whether or not his vocational plans, even if they are very tentative, require a college degree; for college plans have to be made well in advance.) A boy whose vocational interest is a skilled trade and a girl whose bent is definitely toward a business career, will find their time and money more profitably spent at a trade, vocational, or business school, or serving an apprenticeship at their chosen work.

It is well, also, for the would-be college student to think very seriously about whether or not he can afford the time and money necessary to complete the course. A scarcity of cash is not an insurmountable handicap, but it takes some careful planning, hard work, and usually very frugal living to earn most or all of one's way. Many campus activities, an important aspect of college life, are often denied to such a student. Unless he or she has an exceptional mind, or a very serious purpose, college may not be worth the struggle.

If you are convinced that it is, however, don't let lack of money discourage you in your ambition. If your purpose is serious, you will be willing to work for a year and save your money before you try to enter. Look into the possibilities of self-help institutions. Your state university either charges no tuition or its tuition is much less than that of private colleges.

Your denomination may have scholarships for young people of limited financial means. Scholarships, sometimes very generous ones, are maintained also by many communities and fraternal organizations, as well as by colleges themselves.[1] Arrangements can sometimes be made for student loans or deferred tuition.

Certainly a very important consideration should be, How much money will be available during the four years of my college course? You do not need to see all of it on the immediate horizon, but you should be assured of the means for paying your way the first year, at least.

For the young person who does not want a four-year college course leading to a degree, the junior college, for one or two years, is an interesting alternative. The catalogues

---

[1] See Bibliography: Jones, *Your Opportunity*.

of these schools reveal the many worth-while fields in which they offer sound training. These include business, agriculture, home economics, physical education, music, merchandising, and engineering.

The state of California leads in the actual number of junior colleges, but nearly one half of the other forty-seven states have them too. Some are public, supported by taxes, and have no tuition charges. If, after two years of junior college, a student decides that a senior college must follow, a transfer with credit can sometimes be effected.

Most of the skilled trades support their own apprentice programs. A young person is hired to learn a trade under expert supervision and is paid a minimum wage while learning. Sometimes these apprenticeships are served in co-operation with the public school, where other studies are pursued at the same time.

Some of the larger industries carry on their own apprenticeship programs. High-school graduates are trained in mechanical procedures and processes and step into good jobs within the organization.

Sometimes correspondence courses are worth while, but they should be selected with great care and not on the basis of exaggerated claims. It requires a great big dose of "stick-to-it" psychology to see a correspondence course through to the end without benefit of teacher, fellow students, or academic surroundings. But it has been done.

The educational programs and vocational plans of a great many young men are being interrupted today by the demands of the war-threatened world in which we live. Deferments may be had by superior college students, but by far the largest number of physically able young men are called upon to enter some branch of the military service.

Sometimes it is possible to learn a skill or to continue one's education during off-duty hours in the service. As a matter of fact, if it is possible, the armed services encourage this. In the Army, for example, there are at present five general divisions of study in the Army education program, and similar opportunities exist in the Navy and Air Force. *The Occupational Handbook of the United States Army*— issued by the Office of the Adjutant General, Department of the Army, Washington 25, D. C.—lists these and provides full information about them.

When it is possible, the young man who considers his military service a temporary interruption in his career-planning should take advantage of any educational or vocational opportunities open to him while doing his "hitch."

There is a type of education, though not formally so labeled, which no one who covets the best things in life can neglect. We might call it "education by the way," and without it academic and technical training have very limited value. School and college, of course, teach us many things; among them, how to earn a living. Then life itself takes over, with its own variety of lessons. Some of these lessons are easily learned and pleasant. Others are hard to learn and unpleasant. Some of them will be obvious to you soon after you take your place in the world. Others will grow into your consciousness slowly. Some of them you will be eager and pleased to learn. Others you will be tempted to rebel against.

What kind of education will you acquire as a result of your experiences with life? If you are teachable and build on your formal education, life will encourage you to be tolerant, sympathetic, understanding, courageous, and appreciative. And you will never stop learning.

CHAPTER SIX

Where to Find Out About Occupations

THOUSANDS of different jobs, representing an enormous variety of activities—as unrelated as raising earthworms (I know two young women who own a very prosperous earthworm farm) and playing in a symphony orchestra—may be a bewildering or an intriguing assortment, depending upon how you view them. Bewildering they are as they appear in the long listings of the *Dictionary of Occupational Titles.* But narrowed down to fit one's own abilities and interests, such a variety of job possibilities available for every young person of ability and training becomes an interesting project to dig into.

Having decided, at least tentatively, that you have been equipped by nature with certain characteristics which you are now in the process of developing and building upon, you are, or you soon will be, interested in finding out about various occupations at which you might want to put your skills to work. Lacking such knowledge, it is easy to drift into the nearest job.

Phyllis was one of the unhappiest girls, vocationally speaking, whom I had ever met, when we first discussed her problem. She lived in a small city and had what was regarded in her circle as a fairly good job in a local insurance office. Working conditions were pleasant; there was no pressure beyond what reasonably could be expected in a busy office; and her wages were standard for that locality. But Phyllis was bored when she was not harassed. The nature of the business in which she was engaged did not interest her, and she found equally dull her own contribution to that business. Phyllis was a well-meaning but incompetent office worker, and the strain of pushing herself to finish a day's work, with no impetus from within her own mind and spirit, was changing her personality. Psychosomatic headaches were becoming a chronic ailment.

As we talked over her situation, Phyllis reviewed the course of her career since she entered high school, with a view to discovering "How I ever landed in an office job!" Hers was a common story. She had been an average student, and college had not been an objective, so she chose the commerce course in high school. She did not like bookkeeping, but typing and stenography were not too difficult and she "made out" in French and English. "If you didn't go on to college, or train to be a nurse, there didn't seem to be anything else for a girl to do around here," said Phyllis, explaining her choice of the business course.

As a matter of fact there were several other occupational possibilities for Phyllis in her own community, as we later discovered; but she had not had the initiative or the encouragement to find out about them. Even her aptitude tests, set rather haphazardly by a school counselor, had been of little interest or help to her. So the commerce course it was, and upon graduation from high school Phyllis had entered the pleasant office of a friend of the family.

That was four years ago, and Phyllis was beginning to dread the years ahead. It is just at this point in their poorly planned careers that not a few girls jump from the frying pan into the fire to escape the boredom of a dull and unsuitable job; and sometimes in a slight panic at the thought of spending their lives at that job while their friends are marrying and creating homes of their own, they are strongly tempted to marry the first man who appears on the matrimonial horizon. Now the first man who appears may be the right man, but it is a feminine trait to rationalize oneself into thinking so, if the desire to marry is strong enough. An ill-chosen occupation is bad, but rarely fatal. An ill-chosen life mate is a tragedy not so easily remedied.

Phyllis, with appropriate guidance, was able to find a happy solution to her problem; but it was expensive in time and money, as delayed action in planning for one's lifework usually is. She had to accept, temporarily, a sizable cut in her income and take what might easily have appeared to be a step backward professionally. But Phyllis' bent was decidedly toward homemaking and the culinary arts. Since her family did not need her financial help, and she had saved a little money, she enrolled in the state university for a short home economics course. At the end of her course Phyllis took a modest job in a hotel coffee shop, where she picked up a good deal of information about buying, preparing, and serving food. After a few months she began to do a little modest catering. The last time I talked with Phyllis she was a different girl—radiant with enthusiasm over her work.

Phyllis' case history points up two important approaches in the search for facts about occupations open to young men and women today. First, the approach to the *type* of work you will do—in Phyllis's case food preparation and serving. Second, the *kind* of place in which you will do it; in other words, *where* you will use your skill—in Phyllis' case, a small local business enterprise. But Phyllis might have been equally successful in the laboratory kitchens of a large food manufacturing plant, in the cafeteria of an office building, in a small enterprise of her own, or anywhere she could have put her skill and training to work.

Phyllis' experience also illustrates the first source of information regarding vocational possibilities—namely, *observation.*

Many young men and women have discovered that most American towns and cities are ready-made markets for some of the professions, for personal services (such as beauty parlor operators, embalmers, nurses, recreation directors, barbers, pharmacists, restaurant and tearoom operators), for music or other arts, and for jobs in the fields of selling, insurance, real estate, agriculture, amusements, skilled trades, some transporation jobs, automobile service, hotel management, and printing.

As a first step in acquiring valuable occupational information, study your own community and the workers employed there; and talk with those whose careers suggest something of possible interest for you.

A young man in a mountain-resort town was a member of the Air Force during World War II. He had no education beyond that provided by the small community high school, but while in the service he took advantage of the opportunity to take a course in automotive mechanics. He came out of the service at the end of the war with five hundred dollars, a marketable skill, and an idea. He looked about his home community for a suitable location, then bought a small piece of land, and erected a very modest building on it, largely with his own labor. He then purchased all the equipment he could pay for with his G.I. loan, and opened a service station. While visiting in his small community I was sent to this young businessman by my hostess, who recommended him as reliable and as a skilled workman. That kind of reputation pays off, and I brought him a tidy bit of business during my three weeks stay. Other summer visitors did the same. Some day that young man wants to open an agency for a make of car which is not now handled in the immediate neighborhood. In fact he told me that he already had been approached by the manufacturers with such a proposition, but to do so would require more capital than he had to invest. However, the time would come, he hoped; and I have no doubt it will.

This young businessman has gained far more than a modest amount of material success through his venture in his home town. Establishing and managing his own business has given him poise and self-confidence and a place of respect in the community as he serves his customers with intelligence and good will.

If teaching, library work, photography, medicine, forestry, veterinary medicine, the ministry, some branch of science, a job on the railroad, business, a trade, farming, or any other occupation which is or might be carried on in your own community holds any interest for you, talk with persons engaged in that work about the education, training, apprenticeship, and financial resources required for preparation. Discuss with them the duties involved, the variety of work, the competition, the possibilities for advancement and job security, and age limitations. Personal observation and interviews are invaluable aids in studying the wide field of occupations, and from all this information form your own opinion of the occupation as a lifework to which you would bring your best.

It is not wise, however, to limit one's occupational horizon to the home community, for there are vast areas of work which lie beyond the interests of your immediate neighborhood and for which you may be admirably fitted.

A second helpful source of study is the local library, both school and community, where you will find books and periodicals dealing with occupations in general and in particular. Consult the *Readers Guide to Periodical Literature* for articles on vocations. Not only will these introduce you to interesting and sometimes unusual job areas, but they will also alert you to certain aspects of the job that you will never learn in any course on vocations; because the articles are usually written by workers on the job who know the score as no mere theorist could know it.

Other interesting sources of vocational information are the periodicals issued by many of the larger industries and professions. All the major industries, and many smaller ones, publish regularly (usually monthly) a house organ or journal which contains news of the industry, personal items, articles of general interest to those engaged in the industry or to customers, pictures illustrative of the work done, new products, markets, personal experiences of workers, and a variety of timely items. The oil, steel, telephone, lumbering, heavy machinery, building, printing, dairy, aircraft, baking, metals, beauty culture, fashions, construction, rubber, electrical, retailing, women's wear, paper, and hundreds of other industries, large and small, publish such journals devoted to their fields.

The professions have their quota of helpful periodicals

too. Workers in the fields of architecture, engineering of various types, the ministry, law, teaching, medicine, psychiatry, and art are served by magazines and bulletins pertaining to their professions. Incidentally, the preparation and publication of thousands of such periodicals demand writers, editors, artists, layout experts, and printers—a large occupational field in itself.

You will find all these periodicals listed in the *Ayers Directory of Newspapers and Periodicals,* published yearly and subscribed to by many large libraries. If this directory is not available in your community, have it in mind to look for if you have occasion to visit a large city where the public library may have the directory on its reference shelf. A glance at the index to the directory will help you to identify the type of work for which periodicals are available. Find the addresses in the body of the directory and write for sample copies or ask if such are available, as they usually are for a small charge.

Our own federal government offers practical aid to young men and women in search of their occupational place by publishing, under the direction of the Department of Labor, information about jobs open in various localities, the job trends, wages, working conditions, etc. Similar material is published by the Women's Bureau of the Department of Labor and the U.S. Office of Education. Write to these agencies for lists of what they have to offer. You will find very illuminating one such booklet, *200 Sources of Pamphlet Materials on Occupations,* issued by the U.S. Office of Education.

At least two private organizations in our country perform a valuable service in the vocational guidance field. One is Science Research Associates, which publishes, among other things, *Handbook of Job Facts* by Alice H. Frankel. Here you will find over two hundred jobs discussed in helpful detail. This organization likewise issues many booklets on particular occupations and on vocational guidance in general. It will be worth your while to write for a list of their publications and to pursue those that would be of help to you. A second organization engaged in vocational guidance is the Society for Occupational Research. Other authentic sources for guidance are listed in the Bibliography.

If your school or church has a motion-picture projector, you will find tremendously worth while the many commercial and educational movies which may be rented or borrowed without charge for showing to young people's groups. Increasingly, leaders in business and the professions are supplementing the school's audio-visual aid programs by making such movies available. For example: It is now possible, by means of a color film, to see how a large magazine is produced, from the time the trees for the paper pulp are cut in the forest, to the final point when the finished magazine is loaded on trucks for delivery throughout the world. Similarly, the manufacturers of records have a film delineating the entire record-making process, with all the various occupations involved. There are films devoted to the plastic, automobile, photographic, glass, packing, oil, aviation, and many other industries, as well as to the arts and professions. Consult the Bibliography for other films which you may arrange with your school or church to show.

Coming back to the local community, it is often possible for students to visit a local business or industry to note not only the general work done but also the various skilled occupations required; that is, the duties of stenographers and other office workers, of craftsmen, of workers engaged in transporation, laboratory and technical research, advertising, and communication, as well as the work of department heads, managers, personnel staff, and others.

If you are interested in a particular field of work, consult with the member of the teaching faculty who would most likely be informed in that area, or the school vocational counselor if you have one. The teacher of science should be able to answer some of your questions about occupations in the scientific world, and to steer you to other sources of information. The teacher of business subjects should be informed about occupations in the commerce field; the teacher of art or music can give you the benefit of his own experience and observation. Other members of the staff can tell you about the possibilities in teaching, in library work, civil service, research, and other vocational fields.

There are many interesting vocational opportunities within your own religious denomination of which you may not be aware. As a matter of fact the religious field is today one of the occupational areas in which there is a lack of properly trained workers. The church needs pastors, directors of youth work, social service workers, leaders in religious education, editors, and writers on the home front; and nurses, doctors, teachers, and agricultural workers for mission fields around the world. The challenge of this type of service is no less great than the need itself, for to earn one's living by helping others in those areas where they most need help—with their spiritual, emotional, and material problems—is a mighty satisfying way of life. Your pastor or local, state, or area youth director can tell you about them.

Organizations like the Rotary, Kiwanis, and business and professional women's clubs are frequently in a position to advise young men and women in regard to their vocational future, and sometimes have committees whose concern this is. You can ascertain the situation in your community by inquiring of a member or officer of the local club.

Do not overlook the catalogs and bulletins issued by those trade schools and colleges which equip their students for definite skills or professions. In addition to descriptions of the courses they give for preparation in definite job areas, many of these bulletins give some indication of the varieties of skills and occupations the modern world demands, and the educational requirements of many of them. We are privileged to live in an era unprecedented in technical progress and invention. We are privileged, also, to live in a period when mankind is slowly developing the know-how for tackling the social, economic, and spiritual needs of the world. All this means that the occupational picture changes sharply from year to year, and sometimes from month to month. The development of atomic energy, for example, opened up potential fields of employment which will eventually transform many occupational areas and create entirely new areas as well.

For this reason it is not practical to include in our study lists of the hundreds of specific occupations open to young people today. That list would be out of date perhaps within a few months, and certainly in a few years. But there are general areas of employment which remain steady, even though new jobs and better methods for doing them are constantly being developed within those areas. The chapter which follows will provide some specific information about general occupational areas.

CHAPTER SEVEN

Where Are the Jobs?

YOU WILL probably be content with glancing through the first part of this chapter now and dipping into it from time to time later. It is concerned with the general occupational areas—which are doubtless already known to you—and with the more restricted occupations within those areas, based on skills. Many of these are familiar to you.

Vocational guidance "experts" and the various organizations interested in vocational guidance have different ways of breaking down vocations and occupations. The eight general occupational areas listed below are those into which the government puts all the workers in our country for purposes of computing census facts.

Agriculture
Mining
Manufacturing and
    Mechanical
Transportation

Trade (business)
Public Service
Domestic and Personal
    Service
Clerical

There are literally thousands of different jobs within these areas, as you can well believe, for it requires millions of workers in many fields to feed, clothe, house, transport, educate, make comfortable, and entertain 160,000,000 Americans.

The above eight areas call for workers in three subclassifications, depending upon the experience, skill, and preparation they can bring to a job. These three subclassifications are:

1. Professional, semiprofessional, managerial
2. Clerical, sales, agricultural, and skilled
3. Domestic, personal, protective, building, semiskilled, and unskilled

You could easily prepare your own list of individual occupations that fall within the three categories listed. Just by way of example, here are a few:

I

1. PROFESSIONAL OCCUPATIONS

Accountants	Industrial Designers
Advertising	Interior Decorators
Architects	Lawyers
Artists	Librarians
Chemists	Musicians
Clergymen	Personnel Workers
Dentists	Nurses, Registered
Editors	Pharmacists
Electronics—Research Workers	Physicians
	Psychologists
Engineers	Public Relations Workers
Foreign Language Workers	Radio Broadcasting Workers
Government	Reporters
Home Economists	Scientists

Social Workers
Teachers
Television—Creative Workers
Therapists
Veterinarians

2. SEMIPROFESSIONAL OCCUPATIONS

Air Transportation Workers
  Dispatchers
  Pilots
  Radio Operators
Clinical Laboratory
  Technicians
Draftsmen

Optometrists
Photographers
Professional Sports
Religious Workers
Television—Technical
  Workers
Window Display Artists

3. MANAGERIAL OCCUPATIONS

Advertising
  Managerial and
  Contact Workers
Buyers
Credit Managers

Executives
Funeral Directors
Government
Politicians
Purchasing Agents

II

1. CLERICAL OCCUPATIONS

Air Transportation Workers
Bank Workers
Bookkeepers
Cashiers
Collectors
Department Store Workers
Telephone Operators

Insurance Workers—Home
  Office
Office Clerks
Office Machine Operators
Postal Workers
Stenographers
Telegraph Operators
Typists

2. SALES OCCUPATIONS

Automobile Salesmen
House-to-House Canvassers
Insurance Workers
  Agents

Brokers
Real Estate Agents
Salesmen, Traveling
Store Sales Persons

3. Agricultural Occupations

Farmers
Landscape Gardeners

Horse Breeders and Trainers
Nurserymen

4. Fishery Occupations

5. Forestry Occupations

Foresters
Fur Trappers

Wildlife Management
Workers

6. Skilled Occupations

Bakers
Brick and Stone Masons
Carpenters
Dressmakers
Electricians
Foremen
Furriers
Instrument Workers
Linemen
Telephone, Telegraph, and
  Electric Power
Lithographers
Machinists
Mechanics
Watch Repairmen

Motion Picture Workers
  (Craftsmen)
Painters
Photoengravers
Plasterers
Plumbers and Steamfitters
Pressmen
Sheet Metal Workers
Shoe Repairmen
Stationary Engineers
Stereotypers
Tailors
Tool and Die Makers
Typesetters and Compositors

III

1. Domestic Service Occupations

2. Personal Service Occupations

Air Transportation Workers
  Stewardesses
Barbers
Beauticians

Embalmers
Hotel Workers
Practical Nurses
Recreation Workers

3. PROTECTIVE SERVICE OCCUPATIONS

Air Force
Army
Coast Guard
Firemen

Marine Corps
Merchant Marine
Navy
Police

4. BUILDING SERVICE OCCUPATIONS

Building Maintenance
Workers

5. SEMISKILLED OCCUPATIONS

Bus Drivers
Coal Miners

Lumbermen
Textile Workers

6. UNSKILLED OCCUPATIONS

Longshoremen and Stevedores   Unskilled Laborers
Warehousemen

The above lists are incomplete and subject to frequent change. They are not very useful except possibly to supply an over-all picture of the variety of jobs in which people are engaged at a particular period. They also give an inkling of the contrast in the nature of the work which educated and uneducated or trained and untrained people do. Here is more evidence, if more is needed, that the most interesting work and the important tasks are the plums that come to those persons who have the best educational and occupational backgrounds.

There are, however, some very important facts about these occupational areas which are extremely pertinent to your own vocational decision. The first fact to be borne in mind when you are looking around for that job is that *some occupational areas are in the ascendency and some are gradually disappearing*, even though they may be thriving at the moment in your own community.

Among the job areas which are growing and probably will continue to grow for a long time are: the science field, where nuclear physics, electronics, chemical research, etc., have opened up as yet unaccounted areas for study and application; the medical field, especially for research and experiment, in which private industry is investing millions of dollars; and for doctors, surgeons, nurses, and veterinarians; the area of religious education and service, where the demand far exceeds the supply of trained personnel; the manufacturing, processing, and distributing of food; the field of agriculture, where farm workers particularly are in heavy demand, and with the rising urban population they will continue to be in demand despite increased use of farm machinery; the teaching profession, which is desperately in need of recruits in all areas and on all grade levels; publishing and printing, to supply a nation of readers and students with all the general literature, textbooks, magazines, advertising, source materials, etc., that they demand and need; the area of transportation, of both people and goods; the area of building, to supply the necessary housing, short for many years (this field is dependent somewhat on general economic conditions, but a rising population is bound to keep building at a steady level of activity for some time); machine-repair work, to service the radios, television sets, cars, watches, furniture, oil burners, refrigerators, business machines, and hundreds of other items we use; the merchandising areas, where store owners and managers, sales personnel, buyers, etc., are needed to distribute thousands upon thousands of items to more and more people; and the recreation area, especially in the fields of out-of-door recreational facilities and camping and sporting activities.

Clerical workers of all kinds are in increasing demand. This is the fastest growing occupational field because the growth and complexity of business and government require more and more records to be prepared, mailed, and filed. This means that stenographers, bookkeepers, typists, office-machine operators, and other clerical workers can find jobs with little difficulty.

The occupational areas which are on the downgrade include those which have or will become obsolete as new inventions replace them. In some communities the iceman, the blacksmith, the small farmer, the entertainment orchestra, the dealer in horses, the movie-theater manager, and the dressmaker have either disappeared altogether or have seen the nature of their work change to fit an entirely new set of customer needs. Frequently the alert worker or owner switched to a new line in his own field as the market changed. The coal dealer branched out to handle oil as his customers converted their coal furnaces to oil burners; the radio dealer added television to his stock and services; the corner blacksmith shop is now an automobile service station; the small farmer who once raised a bit of everything, today specializes in one crop or handles dairy products; the dressmaker now does mostly general tailoring.

The professional man and woman likewise are specializing to meet the demands of the consumers of their services. Although the general medical practitioner still fills a very important place in the community, the increased knowledge of the structure and workings of the human body has resulted in medical "specialists" who devote their study and practice to limited fields—the heart, the bones, the eyes, the blood, etc.

Our complex economic and legal systems make it advisable, too, for lawyers to specialize in taxation, real estate, criminology, and other branches of the law, although the general lawyer still maintains a profitable practice in communities both large and small.

A second pertinent occupational fact worth remembering is that *workers in the durable goods industries are well paid usually, but their work fluctuates with the seasons, economic conditions, and other outside factors.* Durable goods are those which are not immediately consumable, as food and clothing are. Durable goods include automobiles, television sets, machinery of all kinds, electrical goods, locomotives, and building materials. Masons and carpenters, for example, receive high wages, but their work is often slack at certain seasons; automotive workers are accustomed to layoffs when the demand for cars drops or when some other industries, like steel, slow down for one reason or another.

On the other hand, nondurable goods areas are usually steady, although they often do not pay the highest wages. Nondurable goods include the necessities of life, such as food, clothing, and fuel; and their production and distribution are therefore rather stable.

A third hint in regard to job possibilities is this: *watch for the old occupation with a "new look."* We have hinted at this idea above, when we mentioned the dressmaker who had become a tailor, and the coal dealer who also handled oil. This trend shows up in many vocations today. For example, the girl who wants to reach the top in the nursing field takes a two-year prenursing course in a liberal arts college and then enters the hospital for more specialized, concentrated training. Another girl in this vocational area may decide that physical therapy is the spot for her, and this profession calls for four years of solid work in a school (usually associated with a college) which offers the necessary training. Public health is another growing field for the trained nurse. Hospital management is so new a field that very few colleges offer courses leading to that occupation and the demand is accelerated every year. Medical laboratory technicians are able to get interesting jobs, for which they are well paid.

Occupational therapy is a challenge to a noble career, for some of the needs of permanently injured veterans and physically handicapped children and adults are met through this medium. It, too, is a relatively new and rapidly growing field.

The home economics course leads to the promising dietetics field—in hospitals, hotels, camps, and large restaurants.

Young men and women headed for business will find that personnel work, on which the emphasis is growing in all areas of business and industry, offers new opportunities for working with and for people.

The public relations field is seeking college-trained people whose character, personality, and abilities combine to "sell" an organization or a service to the public. This area is one of the newest in the field of business and industry and the demand for trained men and women is on the increase.

As we learn more and more about the mental and spiritual needs of men and women and boys and girls, the critical shortage of psychiatrists becomes more apparent. To become a thoroughly equipped psychiatrist calls for college and medical school, followed by special study and training in the psychiatric field. A minimum of ten years' study and training is required, but the demand for this service is acute.

Recognizing how successfully the spiritual and mental advisors can work together, some of the larger churches employ psychiatrists on their staff to conduct clinics to serve their people.

In addition to private psychiatric practice young men and women brought up in the church tradition of service are attracted to social psychiatry. This service finds a limited place, in some of the largest cities only, but it will of necessity become more and more in demand by social service agencies which serve the underprivileged and maladjusted people, including the children and young people of their communities.

A young woman psychiatrist of my acquaintance who, as a member of the Bureau of Child Guidance of a large Eastern city, was assigned fifty "difficult" girls by school authorities, had a tough but fascinating career for two years. Each girl had to be studied and helped individually, her confidence gained, her activities directed, her imagination and ambitions inspired. At the end of the two years the young psychiatrist's reward was fifty rehabilitated, alert, intelligent girls. Had she not brought infinite patience, superior intelligence and a trained mind to her job, the results might have been worse than failure; for the psychiatrists' task is a very delicate one. Here, however, is a profession wide open for recruits of both young men and women.

You may, when your education and training are completed, be confronted with the choice of establishing your own business or working for somebody else. As a general rule—unless a young person has the opportunity to step into a business already in good running order, and where he may continue to profit from sound experience—a period of apprenticeship serves one in good stead. The number of business failures which take place every year is very large, and these failures are largely owing to mismanagement. The young man mentioned earlier, who started at once with his own service station, had one big advantage—the need for such a station in his community where the competition was very slight. Even so, he very likely had to profit from some of his own mistakes made through his lack of business experience.

Except in rare cases the young man and woman who have the training and capital, which equip them for setting up a business or profession of their own, are well advised to get some practical experience on the job first, because there are many aspects to running one's own business in addition to the selling or other direct skills involved. The young entrepreneur must learn to buy supplies wisely, to keep accurate accounts, to handle personnel, to advertise judiciously, to keep abreast of the newest marketing methods, and otherwise to take care of all the many problems that arise in any business or professional organization, small or large.

Although one must take risks, meet increasing competition from wealthy chains, and satisfy the capricious tastes of discriminating customers, there are rewards in being in business for oneself. Profits, like losses, are yours alone. You are your "own boss." You can use your own judgment, for good or ill, with no "kibitzers" to tell you how to do your job. For the young man and woman of judgment and business ability, with a background of practical business experience and with the necessary amount of capital to see them through the early years, the single proprietorship has many attractions.

CHAPTER EIGHT

Some Job Troubles Can Be Avoided

THE COMPETITION for the best jobs is becoming stiffer every year, due largely to the fact that more and more young people are equipping themselves with the education and training necessary to get them. Young men and women just starting out on an ambitious vocational career used to be told, "There's always room at the top"; but in many areas of work that encouraging slogan is no longer borne out by the facts. It stands to reason that in a given industry the positions at the top are few when compared to the size of the labor force required all the way down the line to carry on the business. It is also true that a given community can absorb just so many professions and services, superior though all of them might be.

This is not to suggest that your vocational sights should not be trained on the highest point possible or practical. Employers are still looking for superior people to fill superior jobs. Furthermore, in some fields of work there *is* still plenty of room at the top; and your generation will be called upon to fill those jobs. But your generation will also be called upon to do the intelligent, conscientious *following*—without which no big job can be done, which holds importance and prestige in its own right, and, incidentally, creates some very good jobs.

A college entrance committee was recently surprised to read on one girl's questionnaire this reply to their request for the applicant's qualities for leadership, "I have none." Such frankness was so unique in the committee's experience that the chairman wrote to the young woman: "Our college is more than happy to welcome one follower in its entering class. Thus far we have interviewed 294 leaders!" There is a good deal to be said for the ambition to become a thoroughly capable and indispensable second lieutenant, not to say an equally indispensable foot soldier. Without them the plans of the masterminds would never get off paper and the work of the world could not be done.

Whether or not you are ever invited to supply the "high potential" in any organization or profession will depend upon several considerations, in addition to your own ability and skill. Some of these you can control, and some of them you will have little to say about. At this stage of your life venture, however, you will be wise to set your objectives high and to prepare yourself to work out the problems of their attainment, including promotion on the job, as they arise. You can anticipate many of your problems, if you keep in mind while you are still a student, some pertinent considerations with respect to lifework.

Here are some of the questions which you may wisely put to yourself as you think about that vocation to which you are attracted.

First, "Can I afford the time and money necessary for thorough preparation?" As suggested earlier, students should not be too easily discouraged because of lack of funds; but they must recognize that some careers—like those of the doctor, minister, and scientist—call for four years of college, at least two and sometimes four years of graduate work, and possibly internship or long apprenticeship. So the question of money and time to be expended must be faced realistically. If a young man or woman has no family responsibilities and possesses good health, ways can usually be found, through scholarships, part-time work, and self-help colleges, to see them through. Otherwise, some related occupational field, less demanding but still provocative, may be a satisfactory alternative.

Less important perhaps, but still worthy of some thought, is the question, "Is the vocation I am considering over-crowded?" If you plan to pursue your occupation in your home community, or nearby, study the market for it. In most urban areas the legal profession, for example, is over-crowded. Equally discouraging is the teaching profession on the college level. Teachers for elementary and high schools are in heavy demand. Apropos this situation, the remark of a city high school teacher made to a group of teachers college undergraduates not long ago is significant, and encouraging too.

If I were graduating from a teacher's college this year, I would make up my mind to follow my career in the small community, where the schools are less ridden with politics, the classes smaller, the students more receptive on the whole, and the teachers more independent of outside criticism and pressure. The community is friendlier and the teacher knows his students on an entirely different basis from that possible for the teacher in a large city. The rewards of small-town teaching far outbalance the higher salaries paid in the large city systems.

This teacher's advice seems to be another plug for that nugget of wisdom which turned up earlier in our study, "Money isn't everything!"

Another field where competition is sharp because of an oversupply of workers is that of commercial art. There are too many "somewhat clever" people seeking to make a living by means of their skill with a paintbrush. But here there *is* plenty of room at the top, *if* you have superior talent and know how to sell your service to advantage, usually through an agent who will, for a commission, take your samples and attempt to get assignments for you.

If you have artistic talent, the graphic arts field is less crowded and offers many opportunities for your creative skill. Books and periodicals must be designed and laid out by trained artists. Cover jackets, advertising material, catalogues, and circulars must be attractive and original, and the skilled worker in the graphic arts field is called upon to do the job.

Your first practical step toward such a career is to send for a catalog issued by an institution which gives courses in this field. A letter addressed to the Department of Education of your state will supply you with the names of such institutions in your own state, or the nearest available. Incidentally, the worker in the graphic arts must have one personal qualification not always demanded of the artist in other fields who can set his own pace; namely, the ability to work rapidly, sometimes under pressure. It very often happens that a publisher, or an advertising firm, wants a design done almost overnight, and the successful designer must be able to produce it.

By far the largest number of young people pursue their vocational careers within a few hundred miles of their home communities. So, unless you have a yen for distant scenes, the long-range employment picture in your own geographical area is worth studying. Older workers can advise you on this point, and the National Occupational Outlook Bureau of the U. S. Department of Labor publishes data in pamphlet form on the employment situation in different areas. There are definite areas in our country where the long-range business outlook is poor, and others where, for sound reasons, the outlook is very good. Of course distant pastures are likely to look greener than those on the home place, but no young person should hesitate to try his wings where employment prospects loom bright.

Just about the same occupational picture shows up in most of the fine arts. Many very talented young men and women find the field of music, for example, overcrowded and the vocational possibilities limited. Even so, the opera companies, the symphony orchestras, and the concert stage of the future must look to your generation for recruits; and there will be young people among you who will attain these high objectives. Their success will involve unusual talent, good health, financial backing, and grueling work.

Although new discoveries and developments open up new employment possibilities, the rush to these new industries sometimes creates a glutted labor market. This very thing happened when manufacturers began turning out all sorts of articles made of plastics. This situation arose also in the air-conditioning field, and in the intercommunications (within buildings) and diesel-engine industries. If there is a choice, the watch-and-wait attitude toward new trends may be a wise one.

It pays to look with a wary eye at the so-called "glamour" jobs, even though these always have an allure. Not only

are the jobs in these fields limited, but they are eagerly sought by exceedingly gifted people. There can be, for example, in the very nature of things, only a few nation-wide or world-wide news broadcasters. In peacetime the large number of airplane pilots trained for war service cannot find employment. And there are probably not enough passenger planes produced to employ all the young women who, at one time or another in their vocational planning, have determined they must be airline hostesses. Radio, television, aeronautics, and the movies and stage attract many young people who are intrigued by the romance commonly associated with these fields. But the competition is stiff, the training required is rigorous, and the talent needed to reach the top is of a unique variety.

For the encouragment of any aspiring writer, however, here is more cheerful news. Radio, television, the movies, and legitimate theater are much in need of superior program material and plays. But it must be good! It takes time and experience of life to produce material of top quality; but a writing career is a goal for which you may begin to prepare very definitely in high school and college.

There are jobs to be had in the "glamour" fields which not only pay well but are much steadier than those of the people out in front. The airplane mechanics who keep planes moving across the airways of the world and upon whose work so much depends; the monotype and linotype operators who print the news that others report; the stenographers and secretaries in the dramatic production offices; the technicians who keep the radio and television programs operating without a hitch—these are jobs easier to obtain, where the young worker may find his own important place "behind the scenes." And it will be a more stable job than that of the man or woman whose career is dependent largely upon public whimseys and changing tastes. "Here today and gone tomorrow" is not the way you want your career to shape up.

At a summer hotel where he was employed one year, Bob became friendly with a guest for whom he caddied regularly. The guest was in the diplomatic service and held a post in an interesting, but rather remote Asiatic country. That summer Bob decided that the diplomatic service was the vocational spot for him—a perfectly commendable ambition if a young person has the qualifications for such a post and appreciates what is involved. The nearer Bob got to his B.A. degree, the more his misgivings in regard to his youthful decision grew, for he began to look at his dream job realistically. In the first place, Bob learned that the top places in the diplomatic service necessitate almost without exception an independent income, and Bob had none. In the second place, this was a career governed largely by politics, making it undesirable for a young person who had to plan as definitely as possible for future security. In the third place, Bob was advised that it was becoming increasingly important for men and women headed for diplomatic posts to do graduate work at a university school of international relations, and likewise to learn the language of the country of one's assignment. Finally, Bob's dream girl wasn't at all enthusiastic about establishing a home and bringing up children outside of North America, possibly thousands of miles outside. So without too much disappointment Bob changed his vocational plans.

Before you are launched irrevocably upon an occupational career, give serious thought to the indirect demands of that career. Are you prepared to meet them, and will you and your family be happy in so doing? In what kind of community will you live? What educational and cultural opportunities for you and your family will be available? Can you establish a home in one locality, with reasonable assurance of its being permanent? (A young chain store manager of my acquaintance left his company after he had been shunted around between four different communities in five years.) Is a long period of apprenticeship (as in the case of some unions of skilled workers) required before you can earn union wages? Does the career demand a financial investment, and if so, can you make such an investment without too heavy a burden of debt?

These are some of the by-products of a job, and they deserve serious attention.

Then there is the matter of job stability, already hinted at. Some jobs other than those in the glamour fields are hard hit by economic depressions, or even business recessions. The economic situation within a country, or even in the world, frequently determines the supply of workers needed in a given field. In wartime, for example, defense industries are begging for draftsmen and designing and mechanical engineers of all kinds; but in normal times the demand for these workers levels off sharply. Workers in the production and distribution of luxury goods like television sets, furs, and jewelry; architects and others in the construction field; automotive workers, stock brokers, and salesmen are among the first to see their jobs disappear or slacken acutely in hard times.

In short, any business or profession that depends upon better-than-average prosperity is likely to be somewhat unstable; whereas those which supply the necessities of life are usually able to keep the majority of their employees on the job, even though wage and salary cuts may be forthcoming. Despite this somewhat negative outlook, it is true that there will always be, and should be, "luxury" professions and industries, and they must have workers. The better you are, the less likely you will be to see your job "fold"; and the broader your educational background and your own versatility, the easier it will be for you to make the necessary transfer from one type of job to another, if the necessity arises.

It is often desirable for girls to consider the possible barriers to members of their sex which still exist in certain occupations. I worked at one time with an able young woman who had, upon graduation from college, taken a modest job in the production department of a publishing house, where she learned, supplemented by some evening courses, styles of type, the art of layout and book design, and all those technical skills and knowledges that go into the manufacture of books and periodicals. It was, for her, fascinating work; but she confided to me that her future was not promising because of the general prejudice against women in that line of work, commonly engaged in by men. That situation was more generally true some years ago than it is now, and fortunately it is improving constantly; but young women still have a difficult row to hoe in some professions where tradition raises barriers against them. If a girl is prepared to buck such a situation and goes into it with her eyes open, so well equipped that she can meet the competition, most occupational areas are not solidly closed to her. It is often wise to scan the sentiments of a community, however. A hospital superintendent in a small city said frankly, when questioned, that he doubted that a woman physician could find a place in his community, so ingrained was the prejudice against them. In contrast to that situation, I buy gasoline and oil quite regularly from an attractive young woman in a rural village who is the owner and attendant—a "man's job" if there ever was one.

Full of the pep, vim, and vigor of youth, you look upon "middle age" and "old age," if you think about them at all, as periods in the far distant future; and the future can, of course, take care of itself! But it won't, necessarily, even in a crack vocation, although the age at which one becomes "middle-aged" advances every year. So the vocation you enter should be one in which your services will be valuable and wanted, say thirty years from now, assuming that your health remains good. That will be true of most professions and of by far the largest number of jobs in industry. It will not be true of many jobs in aviation and other forms of transportation, in some of the more dangerous building trades, and frequently in the ministry. The retirement age for most jobs of this type is sixty-five, except in the case of the airplane pilot, which is much younger. But if you are attracted to a job known as a "young person's job," be sure that you make yourself valuable in some other capacity, perhaps within the same job area, to which you may be transferred or to which you may transfer yourself when you attain the age of sixty or thereabouts.

The threat that looms the largest in the thinking of most young workers is the blind-alley job. A common complaint among them is, "There is no future here." Unfortunately, the blind-alley job in a business organization is almost impossible to identify before a position is accepted, or even when one has been working at it for some time. Of course the unskilled or semiskilled worker's job is almost inevitably a blind-alley job, because the worker has little to offer to merit advancement. For example, under ordinary conditions the counter man, the waitress, the bus driver, the elevator operator, and other semiskilled workers have blind-alley jobs in the sense that the nature of their work cannot change unless they themselves add to their occupational equipment. Reliable and efficient workers in these areas, however, can sometimes look forward to increased responsibility, and they can aspire to the best "spots" in their occupational sphere. There are, for example, marked differences to be found in the financial compensation received, conditions of work, and quality of customers in different dining rooms and restaurants; and here, as in most occupations, the best workers rate the best jobs.

The blind-alley job is often impossible to identify, because a worker rarely knows what the boss or the department head or the management has in mind; and the modest clerk, who thinks he is stuck for life at his desk in the most remote corner of the room, may suddenly have his job and his wages jumped. On the other hand, he may indeed be "stuck." Who can tell?

Most young people in search of a job make it clear that they want something with possibilities for promotion. That is fair enough, since most workers in any field start somewhere near the bottom, depending upon the skill and experience they have to offer. If you have prepared yourself to serve an employer efficiently, and an opening comes your way, the wisest procedure is to accept it and to give it your best for a *reasonable length of time.* Do not expect an employer to commit himself about your future. If he volunteers this information, well and good, but he probably will not. As you become familiar with the organization and its policies, you can judge for yourself as to whether there are possibilities for advancement. But do not be the proverbial young man or young woman "in a hurry." A widespread complaint among employers is that young workers want quick promotion, before they have proved their worth to the business. In many organizations it is the policy to give an employee a small increase in wages at the end of six months of satisfactory work, but others demand a year on the job. If you like the work and are learning more and more about it, do not worry about promotion and salary increases for at least a year or two. Do not take too seriously, either, what some fellow employees may have to say about employment conditions and promotional prospects in the organization. Use your own judgment based on personal observation and experience, and keep your judgments to yourself.

It is perfectly true that sometimes merit is not rewarded as it should be. It is also true that unmerited promotions are made for one reason or another. But these are not the rule in business; they are exceptions about which we shall have more to say later. Do your own work to the best of your ability, regardless of what has happened to anybody else or of the talk that may flow around you. It is your own record that you are creating; and in nine cases out of ten your worth will be recognized.

CHAPTER NINE

The Employer Has His Say

THE FOLLOWING indictment of young workers in one large city could fairly be made, according to employers all over the country, of most young workers everywhere; and they have plenty of evidence as convincing as this survey to back them up.

Most high school graduates applying for jobs in ———— City can't write, can't spell, can't add, and expect too high a starting salary and too rapid advancement—but they're willing to work . . . the Commerce and Industry Association found in a survey. . . . The survey covered 33,234 graduates, nongraduates and students under twenty-five years old who have had jobs less than five years at the 165 companies participating in the survey. . . . The companies scored high school graduates as follows: reading, 68 per cent; writing, 45; arithmetic, 46; spelling, 18, and grammar, 28. The students did best on willingness to work, 84 per cent. 63 per cent of the companies found new employees expect too high a starting salary, while 60 per cent said they look for too rapid promotion.[1]

Parents complain about poor teaching in the schools;

[1] From *New York Herald Tribune*, June 17, 1952. Used by permission.

teachers complain about the parents' lack of responsibility for their children; college teachers complain about the instruction given in high school; and the high-school teachers pass the blame along to poor preparation in the elementary schools. Probably the responsibility for this poor showing of young people on the job must be shared by a lot of people; but as Christian young men and women headed for a career—in the course of which we shall, for some periods anyway, be working for someone else—let's put the blame right where much of it belongs—squarely upon ourselves. Let's not duck the fact that regardless of schools, teachers, and parents, there is little excuse for high-school graduates making mistakes in spelling (there's always the dictionary), or in grammar, for we have had plenty of opportunity to learn how to use our native tongue effectively. There is even less excuse for any young worker being inattentive, wasting time, and entertaining the idea that he must have a promotion, including an increase in wages, at the end of six months of work. Money, even in a successful business, is not come by that easily.

These faults of workers are serious enough in themselves, but they are usually symptomatic of a more basic occupational illness; namely, lack of any genuine interest in one's work. Too often, say the employers, the one and only incentive seems not to be a letter neatly and correctly transcribed, nor an engine properly tuned up, nor a day's work completed with pride in a job well done, but the size of the pay check.

Now let's all agree, in the interests of fair play, that no one should accept a permanent job in which he is not interested, unless forced to do so by circumstances. Nor should he keep a job if his interest in it continues to lag over long periods. Short lapses in interest can be ignored, for it is rare indeed that any worker can keep riding on the crest of the wave every minute of every day of every year. But more or less chronic lack of interest is a serious malady. It leads to inattention, mistakes, bad habits of work, and physical and mental fatigue. It is a scientific truth that boredom creates more bodily fatigue than physical labor.

Sometimes a worker's lack of interest in his job is due to an employer's personnel policies or attitudes—lack of appreciation of good work, slow advancement, harsh treatment, and so on. But this is not a common situation. Employers in American business and industry are not traditionally "tough." There is usually a pleasant relationship between the boss and his workers, and that spirit of co-operation and mutual help is growing constantly as management and labor endeavor to settle their differences intelligently. To be sure, it is in large part owing to union efforts that employees today enjoy such benefits as vacation periods with pay, healthy working conditions, sick and hospitalization benefits, profit-sharing plans, overtime pay, and reasonable hours of work. But such benefits as these call for a corresponding sense of responsibility on the part of the worker to carry his share of the load.

Your first job may not be your dream job, although if you plan wisely it may be a step in that direction; but whatever the nature of your work—on a farm, in the store, laboratory, school, office, factory—your employer has a right to expect you to assume an interest in his *money*, his *work*, and his business or professional *reputation*.

The young stenographer whom I heard remark airily, as she threw sheet after sheet of white paper into the wastebasket following hastily made mistakes, "Well, it's not *my*

paper," probably would not steal money from the cash drawer, but she was stealing almost as directly as that from her employer's pocket. All thievery does not involve money or forgery. Careless or deliberate waste is a form of thievery too. So are padded expense accounts, and equipment maltreated or neglected. All this sort of thing, far too common on the part of employees, demonstrates a complete lack of interest in the financial success of the enterprise upon which the worker's own job depends. I have heard honest employers, who entertained a commendable regard for their workers' interests, described as niggardly or mean or close by thoughtless workers. Apparently those workers had entirely forgotten that the policy of a penny saved is a penny earned served their interests too.

It is much more satisfying to be trusted, to work without close supervision, than to have the boss breathing down the back of your neck. Nobody enjoys a watchdog. Then young workers must demonstrate that they do not need that kind of surveillance—that they will bring their best skill and attention to a job, whether the boss is within hailing distance or gone for the day. It just is not honest to spend an inordinate amount of time exchanging quips with fellow workers around the water cooler, sneaking out several times a day for coffee, being habitually late, placing and receiving too many personal telephone calls, and otherwise engaging in all the diversions that workers use for wasting time or taking advantage of the freedom many of them enjoy on the job. That type of behavior eventually brings its own form of punishment in the form of time clocks, loss of privileges, close supervision, and sometimes the loss of a job; for when the staff must be reduced, the shirkers and the indifferent workers go first.

This lack of interest in one's work is not unique with office employees by any means. The skilled mechanic is often accused, and fairly, of wasting time going to and returning from a job, or of taking advantage of his employer's trust or that of the consumer who hires his services. The owner of a fleet of moving vans testified in an insurance case not long ago that he had to watch his drivers and their helpers constantly, or they would pick up jobs between their regular assignments, using his trucks and equipment and collecting the price of the jobs for themselves. In the light of such experiences is it any wonder that employers lose faith in American labor?

Finally, your employer has a right to expect you to sustain his business or professional reputation. You may think that he does not deserve such loyalty, but that is beside the point. If you accept his job and his money, you are thereby testifying that you believe in the integrity and worthiness of the enterprise in which both you and your employer are engaged. You will not gossip about him to fellow employers or to others outside the business. And you will "sell" his product or his service with your own belief in it.

It is quite true, unfortunately, that some young people, eager to do a good job and prepared to bring their best to it, have had their dreams rudely shattered by unworthy or short-sighted employers. There are steps to be taken under such circumstances, as we shall see later. But that is not the true picture is most cases. Despite the disillusioning experiences of a few, the vast majority of workers get all the breaks they deserve.

The following "tips" were culled from the opinions of some successful office and industrial workers in representative areas. Adapted slightly, they serve equally well in professional employer-employee relationships. After sober reflection, these experienced employees decided that young workers would do well to keep in the forefront of their minds the following facts of occupational life:

1. *The boss is always right*—or nearly always. It is *his* (or *her*) business, office, or department, and it is to his advantage to make correct decisions. His reputation, his promotion, or the success or failure of the enterprise depend upon his judgment. Don't question it until you are an old and valued employee whose opinions have earned respect. Above all, don't gripe or complain or sulk. Of course the boss is not infallible, but he *is* the boss; and you had best accept the situation while you are in his employ.

2. *You are expendable.* Right this minute (if you are already on the job) there are scores, perhaps hundreds, of young people who would be more than happy to step into your occupational shoes. At this stage of your career you

are far from indispensable, and you probably never will be; few workers are. Employers do not welcome heavy employee turnover, and they are often exceedingly patient; but keep in mind that the enterprise, whatever its nature, to which you are making a contribution could make out quite well without you.

3. *Put your best foot forward*, but don't bluff. There is a difference between doing your best and what employees on the job sometimes refer to as "apple-polishing." Sue worked late to finish a difficult job and laid it on the boss's desk the next morning. Sue made a perfectly legitimate effort to put her best foot forward and the boss was impressed, as he should have been. Jim ordinarily took things pretty easy in the stock department, until the boss appeared on the scene. Then he effected great industry, made gratuitous suggestions for handling the stock, and overdid the courtesy act. Jim was an apple-polisher, to the amusement or annoyance of his fellow employees.

4. *Listen carefully to directions* and ask necessary questions; but be prepared to tackle any reasonable task and try to figure your own way out. It is better to ask questions than to do something the wrong way, but develop initiative and don't make yourself a nuisance with questions that you could answer yourself with a little effort.

5. *Obey the rules of the job.* If the rigid policy of your department is to arrive on the dot of nine and not leave until five o'clock, don't try to cut corners. Some offices recognize "coffee time"; others do not. Some employers are generous about time off; others do not look with favor on such privileges. If you are in a small office or department, personal telephone calls may not be improper; in larger establishments they are usually frowned upon. Whatever

the policies and rules of your job, follow them. Don't play offside.

6. *Learn all you can about your work* and add to your skills and knowledge. A file clerk learned to run the telephone switchboard in her office and also taught herself to type. This meant that she could fill in when needed, if her own work was slack, and she thereby became more and more valuable to herself and her company. An assistant in the technical department of a publishing company took night courses in graphic arts at a reputable school and secured a top job as a result. Employers usually like to groom workers for promotion. It is good business to do so. The smart worker does what he can to groom himself.

7. *Learn to work with and for your boss.* It can be done, and here's how. First, try to understand him. He may be vain, unreasonable, irascible, and even tyrannical at times. Most bosses are not any of those things (except for brief moments!) But if yours is, and you want what the job can give you, look beyond his outbursts of temper, his egoism, and his occasional pettiness, to what probably lies behind it—too heavy a schedule, pressure from above, insecurity, worry, ill health—and overlook his behavior. Second, keep your sense of humor. The number of things in this world which can be laughed off is perfectly amazing. It sometimes takes a lot of doing, but remember that the boss has power to upset you only if you give that power to him. Treat him with good humor (without lack of respect of course) and serenity. If the situation is simply impossible, (and it usually isn't) find another job or determine to do the best you can in the one you have, and let somebody else get the ulcers from worry, hysteria, or ill temper.

8. *If you are sure that you have done your best* and are

getting nowhere, then look for another job; but don't leave your present one until you have found employment elsewhere. Psychologically and practically speaking, it is easier to find a job while you are working than when you are not. You are less strained and have more self-confidence if you know that pay check is still coming whether you land a new job immediately or not. The employer who interviews you may be more favorably impressed, too, for if you are out of work he cannot help wondering why.

While you search for a job, do not discuss your problems with fellow workers. Do not accept another position which will not be a step forward. Remember, you should not run away from one job for another one no better.

You can usually be sure that your job is not worthy of you if: (a) fellow employees are in general unhappy and dissatisfied; (b) you have been employed over a year with no increase in pay; or (c) you have talked with the boss (after a year's work or more), and have received no encouragement for the future.

9. Finally, from the day you take your first job, *set up your goal* and never take your eye off it. That goal should not be a sizable bank account. It should be, rather, the kind of job to which you want to devote your life. Your ambition may be to operate your own farm, run your own business, became a plant foreman, a highly placed statistician, a head dietitian, a minister worthy of his great calling, a top scientist, a construction engineer, or a superior teacher. By means of all the honest, ethical, and worthy methods at your disposal—without pushing others aside or closing your eyes to those whom you can help as you help yourself —steer your studies, your job experience, and your personal life in the direction of your dreams.

CHAPTER TEN

"*And Four to Go*"

YOU HAVE doubtless heard many times a statement, fraught with danger, which is flung around rather commonly by thoughtless and ill-informed people: "It isn't *what* you know, it's *who* you know." The philosophy in that remark is as faulty as the grammar; but like most half or quarter truths, it has just enough evidence behind it to make it useful as an alibi for the person who cannot find a job or who cannot make good on the job he has.

Now acquaintances and friends who may learn of jobs or who can recommend you for a job are exceedingly helpful at times. It is to your advantage to tell everyone you know that you are looking for a job and to make all the contacts possible. But trying to get a job strictly on the basis of "pull" is something else again. No one will deny that jobs are sometimes obtained through influence. Relatives, friends, or politicians who can pull strings are occasionally used successfully to secure both jobs and promotions. Such experiences are so unjust and, like bad news, are so played up, that they create the impression of being more widespread than they are. Other things being equal, the person who has equipped himself to fill a good job will get it. The "other things being equal" means, of course, that there must be a market somewhere for the worker's talent or skill; that the worker must have a personality which will encourage a prospective employer to be interested in him; and that the worker must have the initiative and patience necessary to look for a job until he finds it.

To depend upon, or to cultivate, the mischievous belief that the easiest and quickest way to get a job or to establish oneself in a job is to "know" somebody is a very shaky platform on which to build a vocational career. This is true for three very good reasons.

In the first place, there just is not enough of that so-called "influence" and "pull" lying around to disprove the hard, cold fact that by far the greatest number of workers get and keep their jobs through knowledge, skill, and good solid work. You may already have had the experience of one young friend of mine who remarked, in perfectly good faith, that he "knew" somebody in a radio station who was going to intercede for him in securing a good job. An appointment with this adult acquaintance was somewhat more difficult to make than he had anticipated, but he did finally get an invitation for lunch. The busy man was cordial, mildly interested, and arranged for a very interesting tour around the broadcasting station. And that was that. There were no job openings, and no suggestion was made that one could be created for this young friend. Those employers are rare indeed who will push aside an able worker to make place for a newcomer. And the most successful business or enterprise cannot afford to create jobs for friends of the family.

In the second place, influence, even when it is justified,

may collapse from some unforeseen circumstance. The son of one of the officers of a company with which I was once employed came into the business as a salesman. He was a good salesman, and he started out at the bottom, on the same level with his co-workers. Never was he shown favoritism by his father. In fact we sometimes were inclined to think that the father leaned over backwards to ignore his son's achievements, proud though he was of the boy's selling success and even more so of the friendships he made among his working associates. All the other salesmen were older men; and it was the common understanding that when his father retired, John would become head of our branch office and an officer of the company. After some years the father did retire, and the board of managers of the company promptly, for purposes of economy, closed that particular branch office. John's prospects of ever becoming sales manager collapsed in twenty-four hours. We were all very sad about it, because John was worthy of the position for which his father had groomed him. But this experience demonstrates how flimsy the best-laid plans of relatives and friends can be. It just happened that blood relationship and influence in this case were not enough. Outside circumstances stepped in and changed the picture for John just as ruthlessly as they would have changed it for anyone else. John continues to be a crack salesman, and holds his job on his own merits.

The third reason for not depending upon influence to get or keep a job is that usually such influence turns out less of a bargain than was anticipated. Having secured a job through such a channel, you are starting out on the wrong foot, and it will take a lot of doing to get back on the right one with both your associates and probably your boss as well. The chances are that the boss himself secretly wonders why you were not able to get a job through your own efforts. Getting a job through the back door leaves the donor with about the same feeling he has when "touched" for a loan by somebody who has never demonstrated any financial responsibility. Then, too, an employer who hires people through "pull" is usually not the highest type to work for. As for your co-workers, if any, they will soon learn how you got the job and either actively dislike you or be suspicious of your good intent.

There are plenty of legitimate and highly recommended ways to sell your wares to prospective employers, and these media will leave you with your self-respect and the proud confidence that you made the grade on your own.

In your search for a job in almost any area you may very well come upon what seems to you to be an unintelligent block erected by many employers, namely, the demand for experience. I have had countless young people ask the very reasonable question, "If all employers demand experience, how am I ever going to get it?" No experience, no job—no job, no experience. How can one buck that situation?

First, there are jobs to be had without experience. They may not be in the fields for which you are aiming, and they may have other drawbacks, but any job will give you certain very important elements of experience: in working with people, in taking and carrying out orders, in keeping regular working hours. And in so doing, you will be establishing a record that can be used to your benefit later on. Work of this nature may very well be part time or temporary, while you are still in school or shortly after you have finished school. A young student of my acquaintance worked for three summers as a stevedore on a pier—a far cry from metallurgy, for which he was studying. But his boss on the pier could recommend the young man as industrious, co-operative, and a hard worker. And that recommendation, plus letters from his college placement bureau, came in handy the day he had his first interview with the head metallurgist in a large copper works in his state.

If your school has a program of supervised part-time work, you can begin to build your own experience record in such a program, or in an unsupervised part-time job which you may be able to secure on your own initiative. Go to the principal of your school, to the counselor, your pastor, or a teacher, for information about job opportunities in the community; and be willing to do your best at any kind of job they suggest. Look for a job in local industries, on a farm, in a store, library, or hospital.

Temporary sales jobs are often available during the pre-Christmas rush and sometimes at the Easter season. Farmers need help in the spring and fall; September and October are the big employment months in manufacturing industries. Transportation takes a jump in the vacation months of the year.

If you are unable to get a job for which you receive wages, the next best thing is to volunteer for some work where you will serve the community or some worth-while organization without pay, and at the same time get job experience and establish your reputation as a worker. Remember, *job experience* is as important to you right now as wages, and a personnel manager will be just as impressed by the hearty recommendation of a Red Cross director for whom you worked "for free" as he would be by the head of a department where you earned wages. The fact that you volunteered your time and services won't do any harm to your reputation either.

The organizations to be served in your community may include a hospital, the Community Chest, the Y.M.C.A. or Y.W.C.A., a social settlement house, a fresh-air camp, your church, a medical clinic, the Boy or Girl Scouts, a playground, homes for the aged, and a community center. The volunteer worker who does a thoroughly good job in such a service not only enjoys deep personal satisfaction but earns the most effective type of recommendation when the need for such will be important to his future.

Another approach to part-time job experience is suggested to me as I watch the unfolding career of a friend's young son, who, at fifteen, is an amateur bird-watcher. His professional knowledge of birds surpasses that of most nature lovers who have been cultivating this pastime much longer than he. If his hobby "sticks," this young man will some day be a well-placed ornithologist. Meantime, there are possibilities for summer work in children's camps, where his hobby may be put to work. It is sound vocational sense to "go professional" with your hobbies, for some day you may get paid for it. Photography, decorating, rock collecting, cooking, sewing, entomology, woodworking, and numerous other interests and skills may be the means of earning, at first pin money—and some day your living.

A young woman whom I shall call Jean was of a retiring nature, and in no sense a go-getter; but she had cultivated over a few years a most beautiful garden, small but very choice. While she supplied the local hospital, her church, and her friends with occasional bouquets from her garden, Jean studied flower arrangements very seriously and gradually constructed her garden to that end. Jean's reputation as an amateur with an interesting hobby grew to professional respect for a capable and gifted artist. She won a prize or two at horticultural fairs, and soon began to sell both her flowers and her talent for floral decoration. Jean had a full-time job when her garden was only a healthy diversion in her life; but within two years she was conducting a modest business in her small community which demanded her full attention. Jean put her hobby to work.

So much for part-time work and hobbies. You have completed your training and formal education and you want and need a job. How can you find one?

First, you will of course register with your school or college placement office, if there is such. Then enroll in one or two good commercial employment agencies, if your chosen field of work is handled through such a medium. It is usually impossible to enroll in these agencies by mail, so do not make the effort if there are none in your community or in a neighboring city.

There is a big difference in employment agencies too. Do not register with them indiscriminately. Some specialize in one type of work, and others in other types; and there are first, second, and even third-rate agencies. Find out, if you can, through your school or through local employers, which agencies they recommend and patronize. Your state also may have an employment service you can enroll with.

Study the newspaper advertisements for the kind of position you are looking for. Most employment advertisements are "blind ads." That is, you do not know who inserts them, so a general letter of application must be used in answering. Include in your letter all the facts asked for

in the advertisement, and state your qualifications and recommendations simply and clearly. Do not try to be clever. Employers are not usually impressed either by high-flown language or the "cute" approach. If the ad asks, as many of them do, for the salary you would accept, and you have little idea of the amount you should name, say so frankly and your reasonable attitude will be understood and appreciated. The successful letter of application has three features: clarity, simplicity, and completeness.

It is sometimes worth while also to place a "Position Wanted" advertisement in a local paper or in a periodical devoted to the type of work in which you are interested. Here is one that pulled in two invitations for interviews:

> Young lady, recent junior college graduate, with highest character and scholastic references, seeks modest beginner's job in a personnel office. Competent stenographer and loyal worker.

If you are looking for a permanent job, one you hope to grow with, at least for a time, do not go after just any job. Not to know what you want is one good way to fail. If you can possibly avoid it, do not step from the job family of your choice into one quite unrelated to anything you are interested in, even though you may have to enter your chosen field by way of a very modest position. Dan, a young sports writer, was more than happy to take a job as general handy boy in a small city newspaper office, after telling the managing editor of the paper what his ambitions for the future were. During his apprenticeship, while he performed many tasks far less important than those for which he had fitted himself, he "covered" local sports for his own satisfaction, and at the same time he increased his working knowledge of the whole field of sports to improve his craftsmanship and widen his field. When Dan was given his first assignment, to cover a local tennis match, he was ready, and he did a good job.

The most direct approach, and often the most successful if you have patience, is to "pound the pavements," seeking interviews with all the employers and personnel managers you can contact. Before you start out, type up a brief but complete résumé of your education, training, interests, and references, along with pertinent personal data: your name, date of birth, home address, telephone number, and any outside interests or hobbies. If you are asked to fill out an application blank, you can use your own data sheet as a memo; if the company or the employer has no printed blank, hand the person interviewing you your own, with the comment that it will save his time. Do not burden the interview with too much material. A brief data sheet will do; the interviewer's questions will bring out other facts.

Your personal approach to the prospective employer or personnel manager is very important, but it need not give you any grave concern. Put yourself in his shoes. You would want to know what a young worker can do, and the kind of person he or she is. You have ability and skills which will be valuable to somebody, so you may have self-confidence and poise as you try to sell them modestly. Dress appropriately, arrive on time, and let the interviewer lead the conversation. Give courteous attention to all questions. Look at the interviewer as you speak together, and answer questions frankly and pleasantly. Ask any pertinent questions that you want answered. It is sometimes a good idea to find out a little about the company ahead of time, so that you may make an intelligent inquiry which will show your interest. The question, "How much did you make this year?" or "What are your working hours?" would hardly be appropriate; but, "Do you sell throughout the country?" might be. Leave when the interview seems to be over. To linger too long suggests that you lack decision and business discretion. Do not expect an on-the-spot decision; it is more than likely that your application will be given some further consideration.

It is not unusual for a large organization to ask a prospective employee to take an aptitude or other test. These are nothing to fear. Take your time, forget your surroundings, and answer the questions or perform other requirements with ease. You have passed tests before; this one is no different, and is probably easier.

A "follow-up" letter or telephone call is quite appropriate if you have reason to believe that you qualify for the job you are seeking. One young man wrote the following note a few days after his interview.

Dear Mr. Robinson:

Thank you for the interview which you gave me last week relative to the position in your Production Department.

I know that you will give my application due consideration. For my part, the opportunity to become a member of your staff interests me very much and I should try to serve you to the best of my ability.

Sincerely,

_____

A telephone call, if brief, is also permissable.

Even though you do not receive the first position for which you apply, if the business or organization holds special interest for you it is quite proper to write or call occasionally to inquire about possible future openings.

Whatever your career interest, you can be almost certain that our Federal government, and in some areas state government as well, employs people of training for work in that field. Civil service employees are by no means confined to stenographers and typists. A glance at the list of publications issued by the government for the guidance and service of the American people reveals the very wide area of activities in which the government engages and consequently the variety of experts it needs. Our government is the employer of millions of people, and there is scarcely an occupational field in which it does not employ workers—skilled workers of all types, including scientists in every field of endeavor, engineers, agriculturists, foresters, personnel trained for wild life and fishery service, researchers, recordkeepers, clerks, physicians and nurses, dietitians, economists, statisticians, curators of valuable collections, librarians, teachers, laboratory technicians, writers, and editors.

One interested in a government position should write to the Civil Service Commission, or apply at the local post office, for an application blank which he fills out and returns. If the application is accepted, the applicant will receive in due time a notice of the time and place of the examination to be set for the type of position in which he is interested.

There are many attractions in civil service work. In most cases there is reasonable security of tenure, standard wages and salaries, pleasant working conditions, liberal benefits, and a retirement pension.

Skilled workers in many areas secure jobs through the headquarters of their unions, where, if they meet qualifications, they join the union and receive their membership cards. In many cities this procedure results in a very tight employment situation. A job as low on the employment scale as that of elevator operator, for example, is protected by the union in the largest cities to the point where it is extremely difficult for a newcomer to break in. No union card is available to a man who is not working as an operator, and no job can be secured without a union card—the same old merry-go-round that exists too commonly in work areas today. Before you make plans to secure work in a large city, be sure you know what the union requirements are.

As in all phases of life, careful planning is usually the keynote to success in landing that job you want. Efficiency, patience, perseverance, and your own good common sense will uncover the spot in which you will launch your career.

CHAPTER ELEVEN

Careers in Church Vocations

A FEW years ago there appeared in the London *News Chronicle* a want ad which caused the readers of that newspaper to blink once or twice and take another look. The ad read something like this:

> Wanted: 6 men to take the place of 1, a young Oxford man, who has just died at his post. Applicants must be willing to work without pay, eat Chinese food, dress Chinese style, and live a strenuous life in the rugged, lonely Kansu Corridor of the Mongolian and Tibetan Mountains, serving God and a needy people.

The picture so painted of life in this remote section of China was not rosy, for the head of the organization running the ad wanted no movie-inspired response from restless young men looking for adventure. And so he played up the stark truth, with no beguiling trimmings.

Most of the readers of the *News Chronicle* would have

been even more surprised had they learned of the replies which the ad evoked. Three hundred young men of Britain volunteered for the job. A careful screening proved them to be quite aware of what lay ahead of the successful applicants. These men were not romantic adventurers. They were intelligent, consecrated young Englishmen, prepared to serve God and their fellows in a neglected, extremely rugged area of the world.

This inspiring bit of news is only one illustration of the very definite desire which exists among a select group of young men and women to give their lives, that most precious possession, to something that is really *worth* their lives. So much in life is not. Merely to earn a living, to be comfortable, to amass a fortune, to keep up with inflated and often false standards of living, to compete for place, prestige, and position, and to meet "the right people," are not enough. Such strivings are frequently devoid of love, integrity, good cheer, and other spiritual values. It is easy to lose one's way along that twisted route. Surely, reflect sensitive, thoughtful youth, physical comforts, amusements, and luxuries are not the chief ends of man, his *raison d'être*, even though much of the tone and tenor of our day seems to say that they are.

To a Christian, life is never the "rat race" of the cynic, for he brings nobility to it and finds much that is noble in return. And life reaches its highest level of achievement and satisfaction for those who dedicate themselves to the task of leading men and women and boys and girls, sometimes in needy areas but often in materially favored places, to a more abundant life than they could ever attain alone.

So it is not surprising that three hundred intrepid young

Englishmen were attracted by the refreshing challenge of a way of life at a lonely mission station, where they could give themselves to the greatest and most permanently satisfying business in the world—that of Christian service.

You very likely have heard ministers remark that they had been "called" to their Christian ministry. And it may have occurred to you to wonder what they meant by a "call," or how they recognized it as such. The term suggests some unnatural experience that suddenly changes the course of one's thinking and of one's life.

There is no doubt that God definitely directs young men and women to enter his service as a full-time profession. That must be true by the very nature of the work involved, for it demands qualities of spirit that would not be found in any but the highly consecrated man and woman. When, as rarely occurs, an unqualified person enters professional Christian work—for unworthy or unclear motives—he soon fails either because he cannot face up to its demands, or because he falls down on the tasks involved.

No two people are called of God in the same way. John became a minister because his background and interests as a minister's son directed him toward that profession. But sometimes there seems to be a "divine spark" in a young man or woman who has had no encouragement in the home environment. I am reminded of a young friend whose ordination services I attended one evening in a beautiful seacoast town. As I witnessed the simple but dignified ceremony, I kept remembering David as an extremely active boy of twelve or fourteen growing up in our Sunday school at home. Later he had been a leader in the youth fellowship. He even came to midweek services because he was vitally interested in spiritual things. The unusual circum-

stance about David's devotion to the church was that his parents were completely disinterested in his church relationships and not much concerned about David himself, beyond seeing that he had the creature comforts of life. Now, ten years later, David, having completed college and theological school, was assuming the duties of his first pastorate. Somebody remarked that evening that God had placed his hand on David many years before. And so it seemed.

God's call to young men and women usually consists of several parts or elements. Sometimes all of these elements enter into the call; sometimes not.

First, one's home and church backgrounds often prepare the way. As in other areas of occupational life, a young person's interests are directed to a Christian profession through the activities and experiences he has in his home, among his closest friends, in church activities, and in religious camps and conferences.

The all-important matter of personal qualifications constitutes another element of the call. Not everybody is fitted for professional Christian work. There are very definite abilities and talents without which the minister, the youth director, or the missionary, whose work is concerned very directly with people and their problems, cannot possibly succeed. So young people are "called" through natural endowments, upon which they build a great career.

These are commonplace elements. They do not involve visiting angels nor somber cathedrals. But there must be a third element in God's call, and that is a personal commitment to God's plan for one's life as one understands it. Sometimes that understanding develops gradually. As suggested above—through training and background as a child and adolescent—a decision may be reached in the normal course of growing up. Or sometimes God's call may come with a bit of a spectacle or as the result of some experience that leaves its imprint very deep. Even so, the decision was probably not so sudden as it seemed to be at the time; for God had been preparing the ground all along, unknown to us perhaps.

There is a colorful story in the Old Testament of the call of God to a young man who was to take his place in the written record of history. Like many such stories in the Bible, it has modern counterparts. God spoke to Moses one day as he was engaged in the everyday job of tending his father-in-law's sheep. No lighted candles, no soft music, no Gothic arches, no windows of inspiring beauty were there. Just a rocky Midian hillside near a desert, a young man dressed in his working clothes, and a flock of sheep nibbling unconcernedly about.

But God spoke to this young man at that unlikely spot, where he was engaged in a mundane task; and when God approached, the rocky plot of ground suddenly became sacred. Within the space of a few minutes Moses was called of God to an extremely difficult and tremendously important career; a career that changed the course of history for an entire race of people, and indirectly for much of the world.

Sudden as the final call was, there was far more to it than the "flaming bush" episode. Moses' secular education in the home of an Egyptian princess; his growing consciousness of the suffering and need of his own people; his years of discipline and labor as a shepherd in his father-in-law's employ; his natural endowments (one of which, you may recall, he had to cultivate, for he was not a man to whom public speech came easily); and, finally, his willingness to accept the responsibility laid upon him—all these circumstances of background and preparation were very important elements in the call. Put together, they carved out Moses' career.

Your background may be very similar, and you may have had many of the experiences of young men and women who have entered full-time church vocations. But these alone do not point the way to a successful profession in the church. As a matter of fact they are helpful, if not essential, to success in any career. The final and determining element in your decision must be a compelling desire to live your Christian ideals by serving selflessly and completely, with no reservations, the world in which you live in whatever capacity you may be needed for which you are equipped.

This means that your decision must involve far more than just a desire to be a "good" person, an upright citizen, and a moral character.

Giving yourself to full-time Christian service in the church means that you must be more concerned for others than they are for themselves. It means, for example, that you would welcome the opportunity to spend your precious summer vacation as a volunteer worker in a dingy migrant labor camp, where you would scrub and clean a leaky barn to serve as a recreation center; where you would borrow games and a phonograph and some books and toys for ragged, dirty, and undisciplined children who, shunted from state to state, following the crops with their families, had never known beauty or security or the slightest hint of a square deal; where you would have to work so hard at bringing a tiny ray of hope, a bit of a flame of courage to ignorant, suspicious, but despairing mothers; where you would be criticized, laughed at, or resented by officialdom in the community; where you would seem much of the time to be knocking yourself out to no purpose. But there would be a purpose, as the serene, steadfast, utterly joyous young workers with whom I talked at just such a camp gave abundant evidence.

Under the auspices of a mission board these young men and women, headed for full-time church-related vocations, were trying their wings and testing themselves in a tough assignment. The church, as it so often does, had stepped in to carry on where the state and business had left off. And these young people saw in a group of migrant workers, not pea-pickers to be exploited, but human beings to be served. Material gains alone would never again satisfy those young men and women. Like Agassiz, they would be too busy to make money; like Plato, having torches, they would give them to one another; like Jesus, they would not ask to be ministered unto, but to minister.

We have suggested that personal equipment is an important element in the call to professional Christian service in the church. In most of the vocational areas associated with the church, a personal interest in and a liking for people, all kinds of people, are essential. The person who selects a church vocation will come into personal contact with old and young, rich and poor, the educated and the untaught, the intelligent and the dull. And all must be served as their needs dictate.

Then, of course, the minister, youth director, and teacher must have qualities of leadership to plan and direct activities, to inspire confidence, to lead people wisely and without giving offense, to be alert to new methods and well-informed in large areas of modern life. Notwithstanding his place of leadership, he must be humble, remembering that not he, but Christ whom he serves, must be out in front.

Finally, the man or woman who proposes to direct the spiritual activities of others must possess placidity of spirit and emotional stability. This is no spot for the hysterical girl or the easily provoked young man, noble as their intentions may be. Emotional disturbances and mental conflicts are the causes of many problems that the pastor and his assistants commonly meet and which they must be equipped to help solve. Thus the work of the church demands to a supreme degree patience, understanding, sympathy, and a steady temperament.

There are many areas in which the church needs well-trained, dedicated workers. Your generation is being called upon for thousands of recruits each year for this noblest of selective services. Certain qualifications are essential for all of them, but each has its own unique requirements in the way of personal equipment as well.

The rural pastor, who serves one of the most interesting ministerial areas and one of the most rewarding, manages a one-man band, except as he can and must train leaders within his church. But he must do the preaching, direct the young people's work, often be the administrator of the Sunday school, teach an adult class, promote the missionary program, and be the friend and counselor, in other words, the "pastor," of his people; and very likely he has to help carry on the business or management end too. The rural pastor has a job to reckon with! But his may be an enriching way of life which involves healthful country living, deep personal friendships, and the warm hospitality of friendly neighbors. Nor is the rural pastor as isolated as once he was. All denominations have departments whose purpose it is to study the needs of their rural churches and to serve them through group conferences of pastors, to give those pastors intelligent advice concerning their problems and to help with financial aid, if that is needed.

The Protestant population of America is largely in rural centers. That means that the Protestant rural churches feed into the larger city churches. It also means that it is the rural pastor more than the city pastor who is upholding and spreading the Christian faith in America. These facts bring to the rural church a new importance and they place a big task on the shoulders of rural pastors. All denominations are seeking young men and women who are prepared by endowment and training to fill this extremely important place in the life of Christian America.

The city minister has many of the same tasks as the

rural minister; in a different setting and with more helpers, some of whom may be trained, he serves larger numbers of people. The pastor in the city must be a good preacher, a sympathetic pastor, and an able administrator. He must be prepared to meet people of every class and station in life. He will very likely have many calls upon his time outside his church. The competition of the city is keen, for the city church is not, as is often the case in rural areas, the only social center for younger and older people alike. Consequently, the city pastor has a wider variety of activities to keep his guiding hand upon. Not the least of his responsibilities in this connection is to see that a multitude of activities do not eclipse the main purpose of the church.

The Christian minister, in whatever community, makes deep friendships, is held in high respect, and experiences the greatest satisfactions that life brings to any career.

Whatever one's talents may be, the chances are they can be used to great advantage and for the service of those who desperately need them in the foreign mission field—in China, India, Burma, Africa, Japan, the Philippines, Latin America—wherever the Christian church has planted the Christian flag.

The field of medicine is unlimited in foreign missions, with special emphasis on public health, and the work of dentists, laboratory technicians, and, of course, doctors and nurses. The effects of the last war in the destruction of hospitals and equipment and the reduction of medical staffs have increased the needs of mission fields a thousandfold.

Three fourths of the people of the non-Christian world live directly from their backbreaking efforts to cultivate land. The lives of these people are tragically barren. Foreign missions, then, need agriculturists who combine technical training with their Christian faith. Here is a great opportunity for young people whose vocational choice has led them into the fields of animal and field husbandry, pathology, and plant breeding.

It is no exaggeration of truth to say that the Christian missionary in the foreign field is the most effective ambassador for democracy and for America of all those representatives, either of business or government, who go from our country to live on foreign soil. It was the example of these Christians which prompted some non-Christian Chinese to place over the gate of their village during the last war this inscription, penciled in crude but flaming letters:

Our deep gratitude to the families of this place who, through the thing inside of them called Christianity, have done more to nurse our sick and our wounded and to help our troubled people than any group we know.

If you could spend an evening with any one of the men and women who teach or preach in crowded city areas, to our Indian friends—the first citizens of America—to children and their parents in the rugged lands of Alaska, to ranch families living miles and miles from neighbors, you would hear some thrilling stories of service where rugged manhood and stalwart womanhood combine with intelligence and personal resources to do a big job on a home mission field—another area of professional Christian service.

Most churches of medium or large size have a Sunday school, a vacation church school, a young people's organization, a missionary society, some organized Bible classes for young people or adults, an organized choir, a Boy Scout troop, and a group of Brownies for good measure! Not all these should be classed as "religious education," but most of them in one way or another come under the leadership, sooner or later, of the director of religious education, who is often the pastor's assistant as well. To organize and guide all these groups, or even a few of them, the director must be the type of person whom the children and the young people, as well as the adults, find likable and to whom they will respond. The clever director trains lay leaders to carry on the church work intelligently; but even if he is fortunate enough to find good leaders, he still will have plenty to do himself. He will build programs, conduct training classes, inspire his church workers, be familiar with the latest methods and the best literature in the field, and probably he will very frequently have to pinch-hit for a Sunday-school teacher or a discussion leader; and he will occasionally have to make a speech in a neighboring church or other organization. This is an around-the-clock job, for the successful director is likely to find youngsters on his doorstep almost any hour of the day or night, looking for help or advice or just "something to do." There is never a dull moment in this job, and the rewards make other kinds of success look puny indeed. For what greater thrill than to guide the imagination and talents of boys and girls to the very best in life, away from the second-rate and the shoddy which bid constantly for their attention?

These cases tell less than half the story, for the vocational needs of the church are many and diverse, depending upon the size of the organization and the nature of its work. There must be directors of music in many churches, and few opportunities in that profession bring more pleasure and personal satisfaction to those qualified for the job. There must be church secretaries, pastor's assistants, church visitors, directors of youth work and of children's activities, and, in some large city churches, even public relations men and clinical staff members. In college and university communities there are student pastors, sometimes on the college staff and often serving as pastors of the local church of their denomination. It may surprise you to be told that there are over seventy different functional services used by the church which are performed by either lay or professional workers. In addition denominational headquarters employ business administrators, directors for country and worldwide denominational work, secretaries, and writers and editors of materials published for Sunday schools, missions, leadership training, and general information and spiritual guidance.

Of particular interest to young women are the vocational opportunities in church-related and denominationally supported institutions for the aged, the ill, and for children. Increasingly, religious denominations are accepting responsibility for the care of retired ministers and missionaries and other aged members of the church, who either cannot be cared for privately by themselves or their families, or who prefer to contribute to their own support in one of the many beautiful homes provided for that purpose. These homes and hospitals employ nurses, dietitians, matrons, and others with less skill, to provide the necessary services.

Church summer camps and assemblies likewise must have the services of nurses, ground and building superintendents, dietitians, cooks, counselors, and others. Some of these positions must be filled by persons of training and experience; others provide summer employment and very valuable experience for students.

If you feel rather sure of your desires and your capacities for a church-related vocation, the next step is preparation;

and that is very important. You would not dream of cutting short your preparation for a physician's career. In fact the laws of your state make that impossible. But too many young people think that a high-school education, plus a few short courses in a special school, fit them to interpret God and represent Jesus Christ in this modern world—a world where more people go to college than ever before and know a great deal about psychology, economics, science, mechanics, and so on. Christian zeal is first and most important, of course; but God can use with far greater effectiveness the young person of intelligence, sound education, and an inquiring mind. You should always aim for the highest in scholarship.

> O God, I offer thee my heart—
> In many a mystic mood, by beauty led,
> I give my heart to thee. But now impart
> That sterner grace—to offer thee my head.[1]

The man who penned that verse had learned that the Christian in our day of keen scholarship and amazing invention is challenged to live as a Christian not only with his heart, but with his mind. Your own church, locally and throughout the world, has many ministries in need of the consecrated heart and mind of young careerists.

---

[1] By Harry Emerson Fosdick in *Sermons I Have Preached to Young People*, edited by Sidney A. Weston. Used by permission of The Pilgrim Press and the author.

CHAPTER TWELVE

Christian Faith on the Job

A YOUNG man wrote a youth counselor that he had studied to be an accountant and had been offered a good position, but that he did not want just a "bread-and-butter job"—he wanted to help build the "brave new world." This young man had a noble ambition, but his assumptions were wrong. He was assuming that the brave new world must be built pretty largely through the efforts of ministers and missionaries. He was assuming, too, that he would make as efficient a professional Christian worker as he would an accountant; which might be true, but then again might not be. This young student of high motives was forgetting that the brave new world, or, as the Christian might term it, the kingdom of God on earth, must be built by millions of persons who will go out into the vast world of work on Monday with the spirit and purpose they have talked of and prayed about on Sunday.

It just could happen that a Christian accountant would be a more far-reaching influence for the Christian faith than a Christian clergyman, because the accountant moves in different circles from those in which the clergyman ordinarily moves, and, by the very nature of his "bread-and-butter job," gains the everyday attention of his fellow workers. The Christian ministry has its own kind of witness, and it is a very essential and important witness; but the clergyman does not brush shoulders with fellow workers on the assembly line, at the workbench, in the laboratory, at the office desk, or in the consulting room. That is where the nonprofessional Christian worker comes in. His assignment, and it is frequently a tough one, is to live his Christian faith in his labor union, at the office party, under heavy pressure of work, with a difficult boss, and sometimes with unpleasant or troublesome associates—in short, in every situation which arises on his "bread-and-butter" job.

You do not need to be reminded that if the Christian faith has any claim on our lives at all, it must be a *total* claim; otherwise it is only sham and make-believe. As applied to our vocational future, this means that to the Christian *every* job is a Christian job. There must be no gap between Sunday and Monday. There must be no closed compartment of our minds and hearts in which we keep "in storage" the principles we profess to believe when in the company of people who profess to believe the same things. Quite the contrary, God's call to young men and women today never ceases. He calls them to the everyday tasks of everyday life; in professional Christian service, to be sure, but just as clearly in all other chosen vocations.

The leaders of the Protestant Reformation, which shook the world in the sixteenth century, formed what they called "the priesthood of believers." They were not priests of the church in an ecclesiastical sense, but at work and among their neighbors they were witnesses to their newly found faith—protestors against the evil of the Roman Catholic hierarchy. A group of Quakers coming to America two centuries later likewise made the definite decision to regard every job they entered as an opportunity to demonstrate their Christian faith and to serve their fellow workers in Christian ways. They were not alone in this, of course, but that particular group of Quakers brought to America a very strong emphasis to the "priesthood-of-believers" idea. No need to ask if those farmers, blacksmiths, millers, carpenters, and housewives believed their careers were worth their lives.

In the written record of the church of the first century we hear only of the leaders of that stupendous movement which eventually spread around the world. But it spread because Peter, Paul, and Timothy, and all the others who got into the record, kindled spiritual fires among groups of obscure workers, who, in turn, exerted their powerful influence at the community level, in the marketplaces and working areas of their world where public opinion was, and still is, finally shaped.

So you may be divinely ordained to a "bread-and-butter job," as a nurse, a teacher, a scientist, a craftsman, a farmer, a businessman or woman—and your career will be at once a way of life and a sacred trust.

> A man I know has made an altar
> Of his factory-bench.
> And one has turned the counter in his store
> Into a place of sacrifice and holy ministry.
> Another still has changed his office-desk
> Into a pulpit-desk, from which to speak and write,
> Transforming commonplace affairs
> Into the business of the King.
> A Martha in our midst has made
> Her kitchen-table a communion-table.

A postman makes his daily round
A walk in the temple of God.

To all of these each daily happening
Has come to be a whisper from the lips of God,
Each separate task a listening-post,
And every common circumstance
A wayside shrine.[1]

Now bringing one's Christian faith to one's job in vital, practical ways effects some remarkable benefits for the worker himself.

In the first place, it gives dignity and importance to every honorable job, for every honorable job is, to the Christian, a part of God's plan for the world. Work is required to bring the necessities, the comforts, a measure of happiness, and freedom to God's people everywhere. And in doing it, the lowliest or highest job becomes exalted as a medium for building the kingdom of God. If that idea seems to you on first reading to be far-fetched, you have only to recall how the communist philosophy was spread in America by thousands of obscure men and women who worked their way into and wielded their influence in labor unions, government offices, industries, and among the arts, until communism became a very serious menace to the freedom of our country as it had to freedom everywhere. World revolution or world salvation must depend upon your generation.

In the second place, if the Christian worker relates everything that he does on the job to his Christian faith, much of the humdrum and monotony disappears; and that is not so far-fetched a thesis either. As suggested earlier, our eco-

[1] "Altars" by Edgar Frank. Used by permission of the author and *The Christian Century*.

nomic system of mass production creates thousands upon thousands of deadly dull jobs. I worked for a short time in a book manufacturing plant, and for several days I sat before a stamping machine in the bindery where I fed covers to the arm of the machine. With my left hand I picked up a cover from a tall pile beside me, placed it on the arm of the machine which stamped it automatically, and with my right hand removed the stamped cover and placed it on a pile at my right side. Just those two movements were required of me, hour after hour, five days a week. A moron could have filled the job. My situation was considerably brightened by the knowledge that I was learning the business, so to speak, and would move on shortly to something else. But my co-workers would be there for the rest of their working days, so far as they knew. What has one's faith to offer in a spot like that?

That very problem arose one night in a discussion group of young workers in industry. Most of the members of the group were employed in a huge electrical plant, which was engaged at that time in producing war materials. I recall the alert girl who told us very frankly at our first session:

I get so bored with my job that I'm worn out by five o'clock and I can't wait to get out to the park or the movies, or the bowling alley—just anywhere to get out. Sundays I spend most of the day washing my clothes and my hair. I know my aunt thinks I'm frivolous, but for forty hours a week and sometimes more I inspect parts, every part the same as the last one, moving along an endless chain. It's enough to drive you berserk!

And so it was. But the interesting part of her story came later. We were just setting up in our church a club for young men and women employees of that plant, many of whom had come to the industrial city from rural or small town churches. A few of them held jobs which were varied and interesting, but most of the jobs involved mechanical, stultifying routine.

It is easy to understand why a normally fun-loving young person, drugged during his working hours by such unrelieved monotony, seeks avidly for outlets; and it is also easy to understand why he sometimes turns to the unwholesome, "exciting" pastimes, which provide, or seem to provide, the sharper contrasts to his job. The workers in our club found a better way. The nature of their jobs did not change at all over the following months, but their monotony was lightened considerably as a result of the changes in the attitudes of the young people themselves as they tackled together their mutual problem. These are the ideas, expressed very briefly, they came up with—and they worked.

1. *Do your job to perfection*, even though it has little about it that is challenging. There's a bit of a lift to be had from the very effort to do a job right. It may not be artistic or personally uplifting, but it is necessary, or you wouldn't be doing it. Furthermore, we never earn the right to criticize the weaknesses or injustices of any job area until we have kept our own job above criticism. That is important.

2. *Don't waste your mental and emotional energy pitying yourself* or harboring rebellious and unpleasant thoughts. The duller the job, the more opportunity to think; so think of important things. Remember that you are serving God at your job, if it serves the common good.

3. *Contribute to the high atmosphere of your department* or your room in the plant. Be friendly, companionable, and Christian. The same girl who described her monotonous job to us at our first session met a poser at this point.

The moral standards of her particular room were so low that pornographic literature passed freely from hand to hand and obscene stories were the order of the day. But, as she explained later, trying to do something about a situation like that without appearing to be smug or creating resentment "sure relieved the monotony!"

4. *Cultivate worth-while interests outside* to which you can look forward and for which you can plan, even at the job. Our church club was a big boon to this objective. Every member of that club had something to do, some contribution to make to it. And best of all, they discovered that in that huge factory of thousands of workers there were at least sixty who belonged to the club, and probably many more potential members, who were interested in bringing their Christian faith to their job. Sharing and discussing their problem was wonderfully helpful. Hobbies and cultivating native talent help along at this point too.

5. *Have a plan for your life* to which your job may contribute temporarily but which *transcends* the job. In this connection personal devotions (which over half the group said frankly they had dropped long ago) should be cultivated. Your plan may involve vocational advancement, marriage, further education, or the serious and purposeful cultivation of some talent. Some of the group were frankly skeptical at this point. They had no talent, no time for study, no extra money to develop a "plan" for their lives. But usually when asked, "To what would you like to look forward as having achieved twenty years from now?" most of them had some rather definite ideas, or dreams, toward which they could begin building at once. And as the pastor advised us one night, "Try living a consistently Christian life if you want a plan for your future that will take every ounce of

courage, imagination, intelligence, and devotion that you possess; and it will pay off a hundredfold, no matter what your job."

These were the "safety valves" which not only relieved monotony but served these Christian young people and their fellow workers as well.

In the third place, relating your Christian faith to your job will supply the poise and the power necessary to meet successfully temptations to do the weak and ugly thing. It is fairly easy to build castles in the air. But putting foundations under them is what counts, as Thoreau pointed out, and that is frequently more difficult. So it is easy and natural to sing on Sunday:

> Where cross the crowded ways of life,
>
> . . . .
>
> We hear Thy voice, O Son of Man!

Then at the crowded crossways we are suddenly confronted with perplexing, contradicting, and extremely difficult situations; for life at the crossways is usually not composed of the good and the bad, sharply etched in white and black; it is more likely to be, at least in the society in which your career will take you, shaded from white to gray. Sometimes right and wrong are easily distinguished; often they are not. Some vocations have their own unique brand of temptations, and some temptations are common to occupational life in general. The pure black variety of sin is easy to spot. Gambling, gossiping, shirking, dishonesty in all forms —the Christian worker takes a stand against these with no questions in his own mind as to whether they are right or wrong, although it may take courage, for example, to stand out against a popular office or department number pool or widespread betting on the World Series. Here again, it is the over-all attitude and character of the Christian worker that wins for him friends and genuine popularity.

It is worth remembering that when we are tempted to say that we cannot be popular or make friends without joining the crowd in any practice which would cause us to lower our banners, we are *really* saying that we lack those qualities of character and personality which makes a person attractive and companionable in any group worthy of our friendship. No worker, if his attitudes are kindly, has to depend upon anything as superficial as drinking, gambling, and other questionable habits to find his place. Among intelligent people personal tastes and convictions are accepted without comment; and, eventually, in any situation a young man or woman demonstrates vocational ability and true friendship by means of good workmanship, loyalty, tolerance, and kindness that goes far beyond the call of duty. We can make our own successful way, socially and vocationally, without hauling down our colors.

Incidentally, since much is expected and required of the Christian who endeavors to make his job Christian, a forthright stand, not spoiled by any attitude of self-righteous disapproval or smugness, encourages others with less determination to follow suit.

Then there are those hateful "garden-variety" type of temptations that plague us all and which are sometimes as harmful as the more spectacular sins. For example, there is the inclination which prevails in any organization of many workers to gossip, to indulge in pettiness, or in office politics. "Let office chicanery and gossip float around you," one very wise department head advised a group of girls in her office. I have noticed repeatedly that the gossip mon-

gers and the job politicians are likely to be those who, for one reason or another, are dissatisfied with their jobs or feel inferior on them. This is another strong plug for finding the proper job in the first place. A stenographer, for example, takes little interest in her work because she is thinking too much about finding a husband. A bank clerk has no natural aptitudes for his clerical occupation. So out of boredom or self-pity these unhappy workers indulge in "juicy" gossip to relieve their boredom, in "politicking" for promotion, or they "take it out" on a fellow worker. Granted that there are jealous workers, gossips, and trouble-makers in many organizations, the fellow or girl who does a good job, minds his own business, and demonstrates genuine friendship, usually makes out all right.

Some of you will be the employers and the bosses in the vocational world of tomorrow. In that capacity you will have the well-being of several, and possibly hundreds or thousands, of your fellow men and women in your hands. The responsibilities and the privileges of the Christian employer are great—to avoid putting stumbling blocks in the path of the weak, to put people first and profits second, to lead the parade in movements for workers' benefits, and to set the Christian tone of the department or office or the entire industry. For it is not enough that a Christian employer be honest. As a member of the priesthood of believers he must be humble; he must be willing to accord to others, employees included, the same right to their own opinions that he wants for himself; he must provide security of jobs insofar as that is humanly possible; and he must see that every worker gets the breaks he deserves. Above all, he will have the Christian's respect for the worker as an *individual*, a child of God, a fellow brother in the spiritual community. He will, in short, make it easier, rather than more difficult, for his employees to exercise their Christian faith on the job.

Now those objectives are easily recited in glib fashion, but the pressure of many forces brought to bear upon the modern employer frequently makes his task extremely difficult. For example, a frequent trouble spot for both worker and owner in our economic society is the labor union. Strikes, boycotts, dishonest leadership, disservice to the public, union "rigging," unreasonable demands—these grievances often justify the employer's and the public's criticism of unions in general. What will your own attitude as an employer or as a union member be? In other words, how can one put Christian faith to work here? There are a few Christian policies that apply to both management and labor in their union relationships.

First, seek intelligently to *obtain the facts* on both sides of the case. If a union member, exercise your right to speak and vote as your conscience and your *intelligence* dictate. Now that isn't always easy. Bad leadership or a majority against you drowns out your voice, rebuffs your attempts, or threatens you with expulsion or even, in extreme cases, physical violence. But if you have the facts, seek out others who believe as you do or who have an open mind, and work together patiently to make your union what it ought to be. The forces of evil are always strong on organization; the forces for right must be also.

Students-in-industry who worked in one particular plant reported:

In one instance at least, their very interest in the union made them suspect by union leaders who were not used to workers who wanted to attend meetings and inquire about what was going on. . . .

Students in one plant reported a great reliance of the workers on the union to look out for their welfare but almost complete disinterest in union meetings. Students reported that union leadership was often intelligent and articulate on political and social matters but that the rank and file was poorly informed. . . .

"From the men with whom I worked," reported one student, "I judge that there is a widespread ignorance of democratic processes. The workers complained because their union is dominated by a clique and because there is corruption in government. But they do not see themselves in any way responsible for these. They have no feeling of being a part of or having a voice in our government. They don't feel their vote counts for much and it doesn't matter much whether they vote or not."

One student with a skilled trade and considerable experience prior to the summer, reported that "working with men of various skilled trades I have observed: 1. profuse profanity and vulgarity. . . . 2. a disappointing disregard of any moral compulsion to deliver an hour's work for an hour's pay; 3. a too frequent disdain of supervisors perhaps best expressed as 'why should we work to make a living for *him?*'; and 4. with increasing age, a distrust of younger workers and an attitude of, 'I'm through working fast and working overtime. All I want to do is make enough to get by.' " [1]

In the case of management, to seek out the facts is likewise very essential. There has been too much unreasoning, bitter, prejudiced criticism against workers who, as a matter of fact, have been forced by industrial methods over the years to seek protection in organization. The Christian employer will do well to remember that it was the great Wesleyan Methodist movement in England that first inspired intelligent, consecrated men to rebel against a government edict that forbade union membership among workers. These supporters of labor were Christian men who were willing to be deported in chains on a prison ship, for seven years of exile, rather than submit to unjust treatment of laboring men and women. The Christian employer today, looking for facts, will study the history of the labor movement, and he will discover that it arose largely because of the blindness, the lack of social responsibility, and frequently the inhumanity of industrial management. Evils have arisen within the labor unions, to be sure, but today's employers are simply paying the price for the sins of early generations of owners. So the Christian employer must not only learn all the facts concerning union demands in his organization, but must place his labor problem in its proper place within this historical pattern. Such a perspective frequently changes one's viewpoint.

Second, *seek a solution of the problem*, or obviate it, through *Christian methods* and *practices*, on the part of

[1] From the *Report of the New Haven Students-in-Industry Project,* 1952.

both management and labor. If you become a union member you cannot, as a Christian worker, condone planned dishonesty, by means of which workers agree to do poor work, overcharge, circumvent a contract, etc., even, as sometimes happens, with the connivance of the management which has its own axe to grind. Read what one group of students-in-industry reported:

> We started out feeling that our primary obligation in an industrial plant was to do an "honest day's work." As soon as we tried it, we found there were agreed limits among the workers themselves about the pace of that work. They were on guard against speeding up, and their only safeguard was to regulate their work to a good job—trot pace and to hold to it by common agreement. . . .
> Several of our people were in steel plants, engaged in checking the weight of molten metal. This should have coincided with the weight of scrap metal that went into the melting. . . . But it never did coincide, because for months it had been the custom—by agreement throughout all the departments concerned—to enter, not the weight which the scales in fact showed, but an artificial figure supplied by the scrap-metal department. The checker's job, that is to say, was not to tell the truth but to keep the peace. Their work was not only unnecessary but invidious and deceptive. Yet, for twenty-four hours a day, six days a week, men and women "worked" and drew wages for doing a job worth less than nothing. To question the procedure, however . . . would mean at least unpopularity and possibly being fired, since in many such instances owners and managers prefer that things run along quietly rather than face a general shakeup.[2]

No simple principle will cover situations like these. They require the devoted, intelligent, long-range efforts of many

[2] Alexander Miller, *Christian Faith and My Job*—"A Haddam House Book," (Association Press, publisher, 1946). Used by permission of the Edward W. Hazen Foundation.

workers. Here is one of the most difficult "frontiers" of American life challenging Christian youth, in their bread-and-butter jobs, to conquer.

Perplexing questions of Christian behavior are by no means confined to the world of labor. The professions have their share too. For example, I was told by a physician that in the early days of his medical career he had been employed by a large city department store. Among his duties was passing upon the physical fitness of employees. One day his employer came to him with the bold-faced request that he give an unsatisfactory "bill of health" to an employee whom they wanted to get rid of without firing! Here was a "black and white" type of temptation. The decision was not easy for a young physician with a family; but there could be only one answer, and this young professional man refused to comply with the despicable request. The result was that he, rather than the innocent employee whose health he was checking, lost his job.

Some problems peculiar to professional life are not so easily solved in the light of Christian faith and the society in which we live. What of the teacher who is discouraged from teaching the truth; the reporter who is expected to "slant" his news story; the artist who must prostitute his talent to make "both ends meet" economically; the doctor who must work in a community where, it is frankly conceded, good medical care cannot be paid for by large segments of its people; the lawyer who cannot make a decent living if he accepts only those cases calling for sound legal reasoning and the support of justice; the government official who is expected to "kick back" part of his salary to a political organization?

As Christian workers in any capacity, we must face frankly

the fact that our faith and the world of jobs are frequently in conflict. To reconcile the two is the stupendous task of the "priesthood." And it requires, as we have seen, high intelligence, deep consecration often involving self-sacrifice, and group participation whenever possible in long-range planning and effort.

The over-all objective of all Christian vocational life, beyond that of making a living, is to make one's career constructively Christian. It is clear that most vocations are neither actively constructive, spiritually speaking, nor actively destructive. They are neutral, carried on for the most part for private gain. Then it is up to the Christian worker and owner to make the organization or the job spiritually high. It is a fact of occupational life that most jobs, if not worked at to that end, will drop to low standards; for it is no more possible to sit on a spiritual or moral fence in this than in other areas of life. No job remains "neutral" very long. The endless struggle for profits, the keen competition, the desire for place and prestige, the race to "get on"— all these and many other elements combine to pull the standards of industrial and professional life down, unless workers on all levels, from the top to the bottom, seek earnestly to hold them up. That is the great task of the Christian.

We have only touched upon the hurdles that the worker will come upon as he brings his faith to his job. Some of these hurdles will be set up by those from whom he might expect help; some by those who are frankly inimical; some by the indifferent.

A high-school teacher who had seen hundreds of young people heading for their life work paid this tribute to the "dream-possessed" among them.

I cannot help but love the knight who goes
Unchampioned, derided by his foes
And friends, to seek the white star of his dream
In the black night. He only sees the gleam,
And, heeding neither laughter nor the sneers
Of sane complacency, his course he steers
Into the starless skies. Perchance for him
The gleam will never out of darkness swim.
Yet better, dream-possessed, to falter down
In failure, than to snicker like a clown
Over the dream. God give us grace to see
The grandeur in the soul of errantry.[3]

Yes, better to falter down in failure than to cast aside the dream; but that young man and woman of courage, intelligence, and the divine urge to greatness never fails. You are headed for the Great Adventure—a career which will be worth your life. Train your sights upon the stars.

[3] Used by permission of the author, Florence Ripley Mastin.

Bibliography

CHAPTER I

Adams, Clifford R. *Looking Ahead to Marriage.* Chicago: Science Research Associates, 1949.

Church, Virginia, and Ellis, Francis C. *To Meet the Day.* New York and Nashville: Abingdon-Cokesbury Press, 1953.

Jones, E. Stanley. *Victorious Living.* New York and Nashville: Abingdon-Cokesbury Press, 1936.

Kirkendall, Lester A., and Osborne, Ruth F. *Dating Days.* Chicago: Science Research Associates, 1949. (booklet)

CHAPTER II

Dobyns, William R. *The Challenge of Jesus Christ to This Generation.* Louisville: Presbyterian Church in the U.S.A., n.d. (leaflet)

Dun, Angus. *What Shall I Do with My Life?* New York: The National Council of the Churches of Christ in the U.S.A., n.d. (leaflet)

Rupert, Hoover. *Your Life Counts.* New York and Nashville: Abingdon-Cokesbury Press, 1950.

CHAPTER III

Bro, Margueritte. *Let's Talk About You.* New York: Doubleday & Company, 1945.

Menninger, William C. *Understanding Yourself.* Chicago: Science Research Associates, 1948. (booklet)

Richmond, W. V. *Making the Most of Your Personality.* New York: Rinehart & Company, n.d.

Seashore, H G. *All of Us Have Troubles.* New York: Association Press, n.d.

Ullman, Frances. *Girl Alive!* Cleveland: World Publishing Company, 1947.

CHAPTER IV

Bahm, Archie. *What's Ahead for Me?* Austin: The Hogg Foundation, University of Texas, n.d.

Morris, Mark. *Career Opportunities*. Washington, D. C.: Progress Press, 1946.

CHAPTER V

Jones, Theodore S. *Your Opportunity*. P. O. Box 41, Milton, Mass.: 1942.

Lovejoy, Clarence E. *Complete Guide to Colleges and Universities*. New York: Simon & Schuster, 1948.

Orchard, Norris Ely. *How to Study*. Windsor, Conn.: Loomis School, n.d.

Warner, W. Lloyd, and Havighurst, Robert J. *Should You Go to College?* Chicago: Science Research Associates, n.d. (booklet)

Weinland, James O. *How to Study*. New York: Office of the Dean of Admissions, New York University, Washington Square Branch, 1953.

CHAPTER VII

Ligenfelter, Mary R., and Kitson, Harry D. *Vocations for Girls*. New York: Harcourt, Brace & Co., 1951.

McCausland, Elizabeth. *Careers in the Arts*. New York: John Day Company, 1950.

Morris, Mark. *Career Opportunities*. Washington, D. C.: Progress Press, 1946.

Occupational Briefs. (Four to six publications each month. These cover job information in all areas and are kept up-to-date. They are available as part of guidance service to schools and other groups.) Chicago: Science Research Associates.

CHAPTER VIII

Alsop, G. F., and McBridge, M. F. *She's Off to Work*. New York: Vanguard Press, 1940.

Chapman, Paul. *Your Personality and Your Job*. Chicago: Science Research Associates, n.d. (booklet)

Wolfbein, Seymour L., and Goldstein, Harold. *Our World of Work*. Chicago: Science Research Associates, n.d. (booklet)

CHAPTER IX

Survey of High School Graduates on the Job. Commerce and Industry Association of New York.

CHAPTER X

Dreese, Mitchell. *How to Get the Job*. Chicago: Science Research Associates, 1949. (booklet)

CHAPTER XI

Lingle, Walter L. *Preparing for the Ministry*. Louisville: Presbyterian Church in the U.S.A., 1940.

Marquess, William H. *The Ministry: A Challenge and an Appeal*. Louisville: Presbyterian Church in the U.S.A., 1940.

Nelson, John O. *We Have This Ministry*. New York: Federal Council of Churches of Christ, 1946.

Wood, Violet. *In the Direction of Dreams*. New York: Friendship Press, 1949.

CHAPTER XII

Hoslette, Schuyler, ed. *Human Factors in Management*. Parkville, Mo.: Park College Press, 1946.

Miller, Alexander. *Christian Faith and My Job*. New York: Association Press, 1946.

Mould, Ralph. *Christianity Where Men Work*. New York: Friendship Press, 1947.

Oxnam, G. Bromley. *Labor and Tomorrow's World*. New York and Nashville: Abingdon-Cokesbury Press, 1945.

McCarthy, Raymond G. *Facts About Alcohol*. Chicago: Science Research Associates, 1951. (booklet)

Yoder, Dale. *You and Unions*. Chicago: Science Research Associates, n.d. (booklet)

VISUAL AID SOURCES

The films listed give general guidance in the selection of vocations, and the distributors named supply films showing the kind of work done by many different types of workers in a given industry. They may be rented from the distributors. A few will be sent to schools and other youth groups for a modest service charge.

Films

"Careers for Girls" (March of Time), distributed by McGraw-Hill Film Service, 330 West 42nd St., New York 18, N. Y.

"Choosing Your Occupations," Coronet Films, 65 East Water St., Chicago 1, Ill.

"Journey into Medicine," United World, 1445 Park Ave., New York 29, N.Y.

Distributors

Allis-Chalmers Manufacturing Co., Milwaukee 1, Wis.

American Telephone and Telegraph Company, Film Rental Display Division, 195 Broadway, New York 7, N.Y.

Association Films, 347 Madison Ave., New York 17, N.Y.

Bethlehem Steel Company, Bethlehem, Pa.

Canadian Pacific Railway, Madison Ave. and 44th St., New York 17, N.Y.

General Electric Company, Visual Education Service, 570 Lexington Ave., New York 22, N.Y.

General Motors Corporation, Dept. of Public Relations, Distribution Section, 3044 West Grand Blvd., Detroit 2, Mich.

Owens-Illinois Glass Company, Toledo 1, O.

Shell Oil Company, Public Relations Dept., 50 West 50th St., New York 20, N.Y.

Swift & Company, Public Relations Dept., Union Stock Yards, Chicago 9, Ill.

United Air Lines, United Air Lines Bldg., Chicago 38, Ill.

Write to the Department of Education of your state for further sources.

Index